RELAXATION SERIES:
COLORING BOOK 1

INTRODUCTION

In our work life and daily living activities we come across a lot of stress and anxiety resulting in several diseases and disorders. It is believed that creative therapies such as art, drawing, and coloring can help us fight stress and anxiety in our lives.

Coloring also provides increase in creativity, brain functioning, and reduces stress hormones helping us to relax.

Coloring helps in changing our mood and brings joy to those who like to be creative but has very less time and a stressful life.

This book has a number of figures which can be used for coloring even if the individual does not know how to draw or does not have the time to draw and then color it.

This book also provides a color wheel so that if desired you can follow the proper coloring method. Every figure/design has a following page plain

This book can be used for both adults and kids about 8 year of age.

Enjoy you time coloring….and release your creativity.

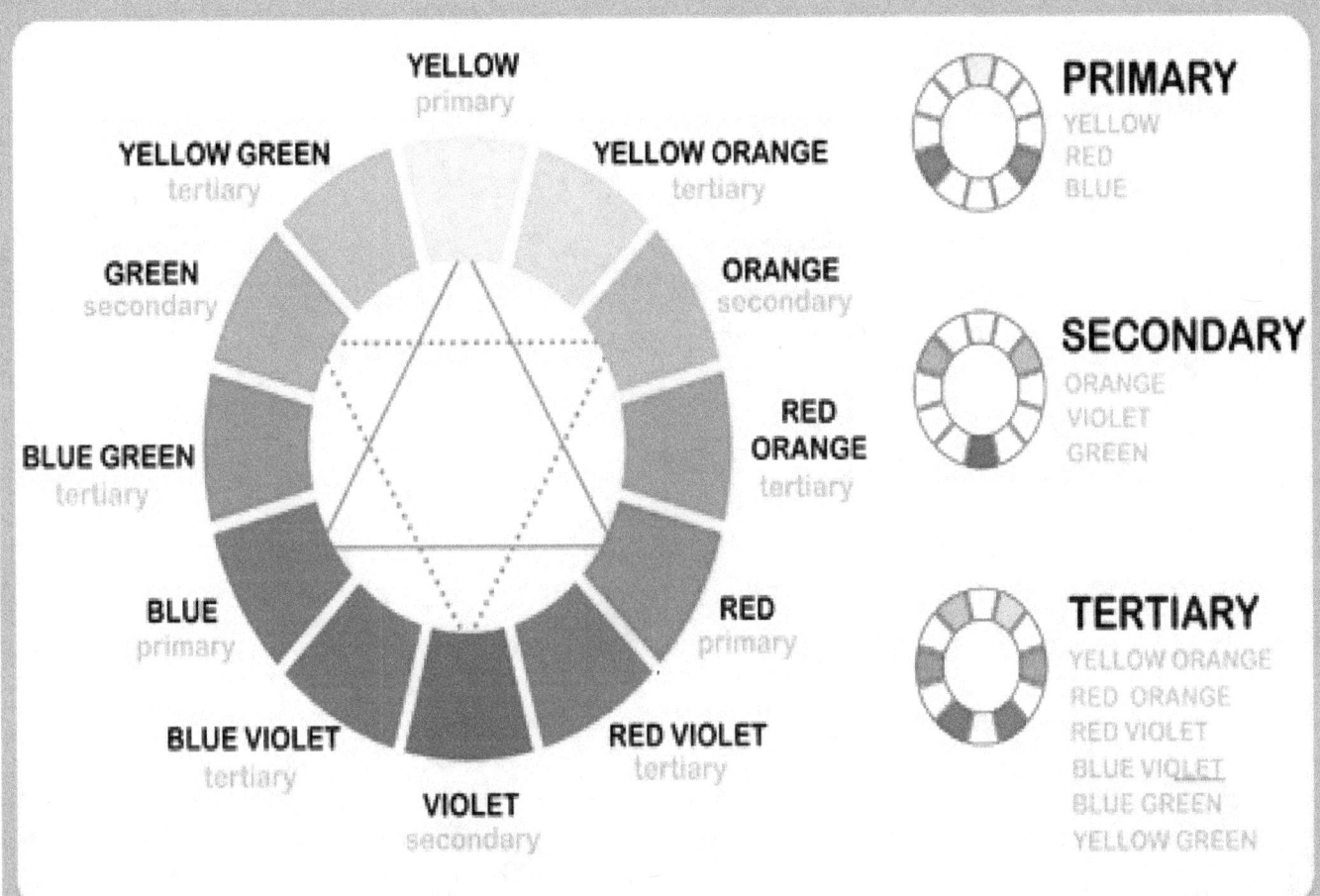

YELLOW
primary

YELLOW GREEN
tertiary

YELLOW ORANGE
tertiary

GREEN
secondary

ORANGE
secondary

BLUE GREEN
tertiary

RED
ORANGE
tertiary

BLUE
primary

RED
primary

BLUE VIOLET
tertiary

RED VIOLET
tertiary

VIOLET
secondary

PRIMARY
YELLOW
RED
BLUE

SECONDARY
ORANGE
VIOLET
GREEN

TERTIARY
YELLOW ORANGE
RED ORANGE
RED VIOLET
BLUE VIOLET
BLUE GREEN
YELLOW GREEN

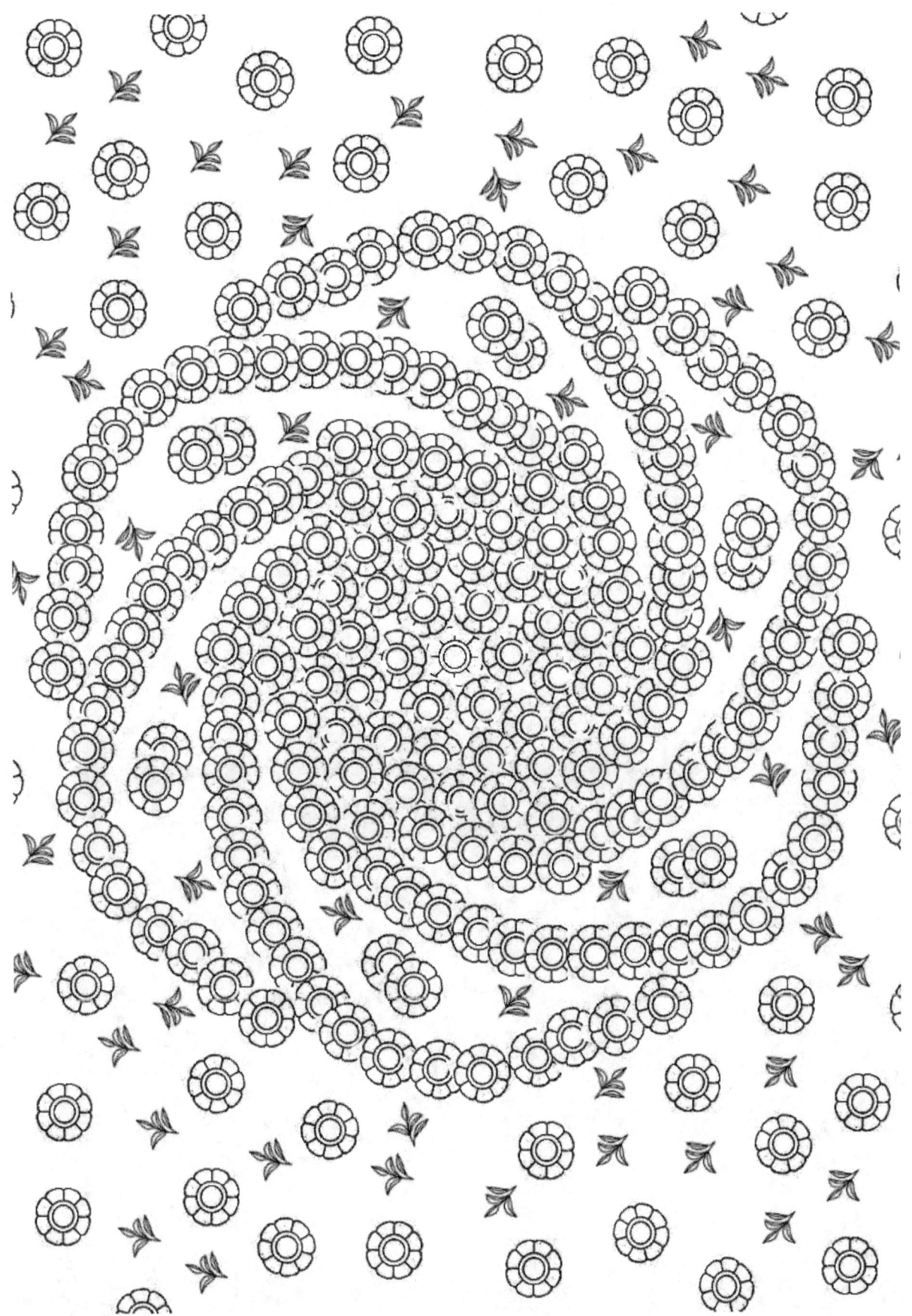

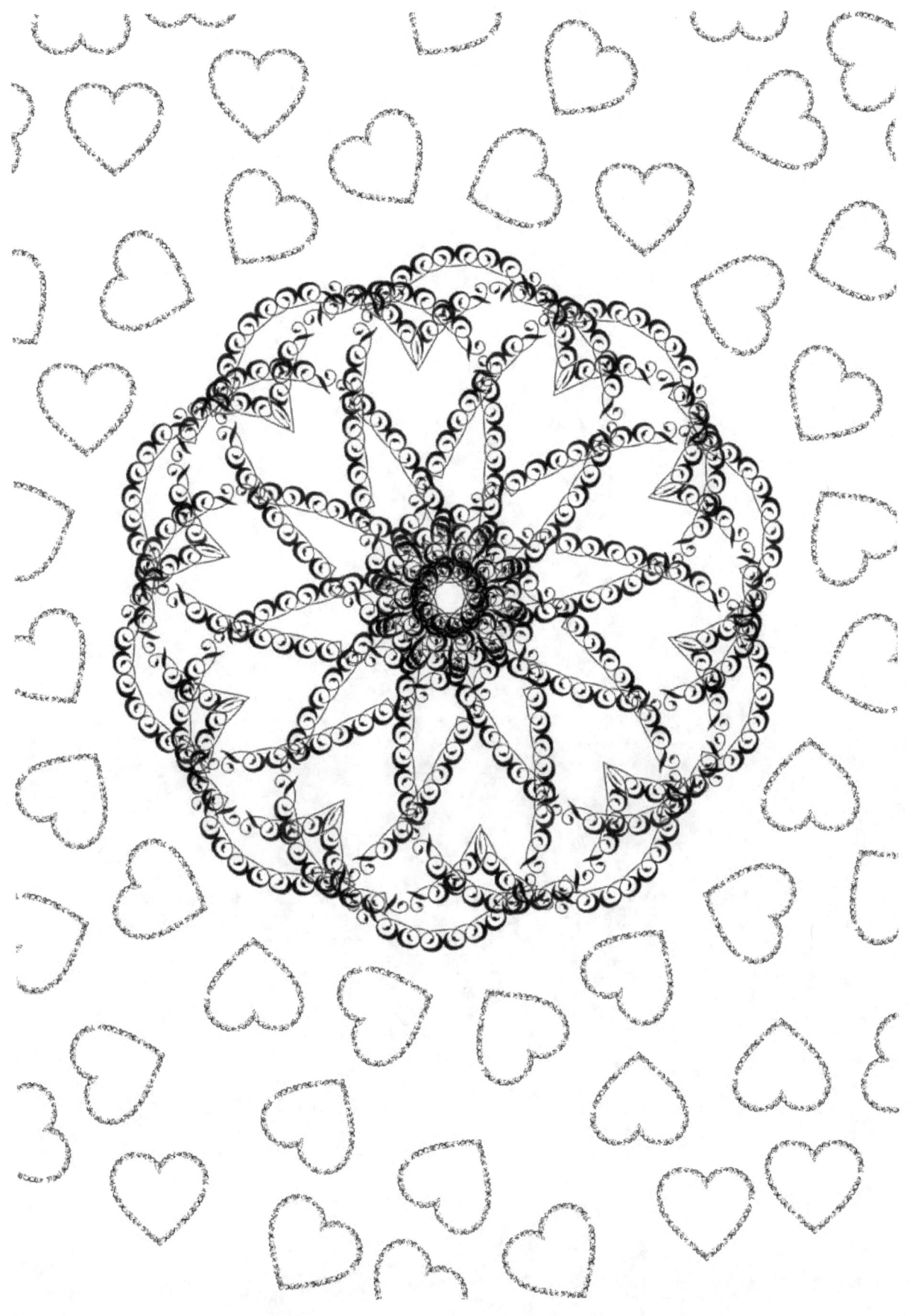

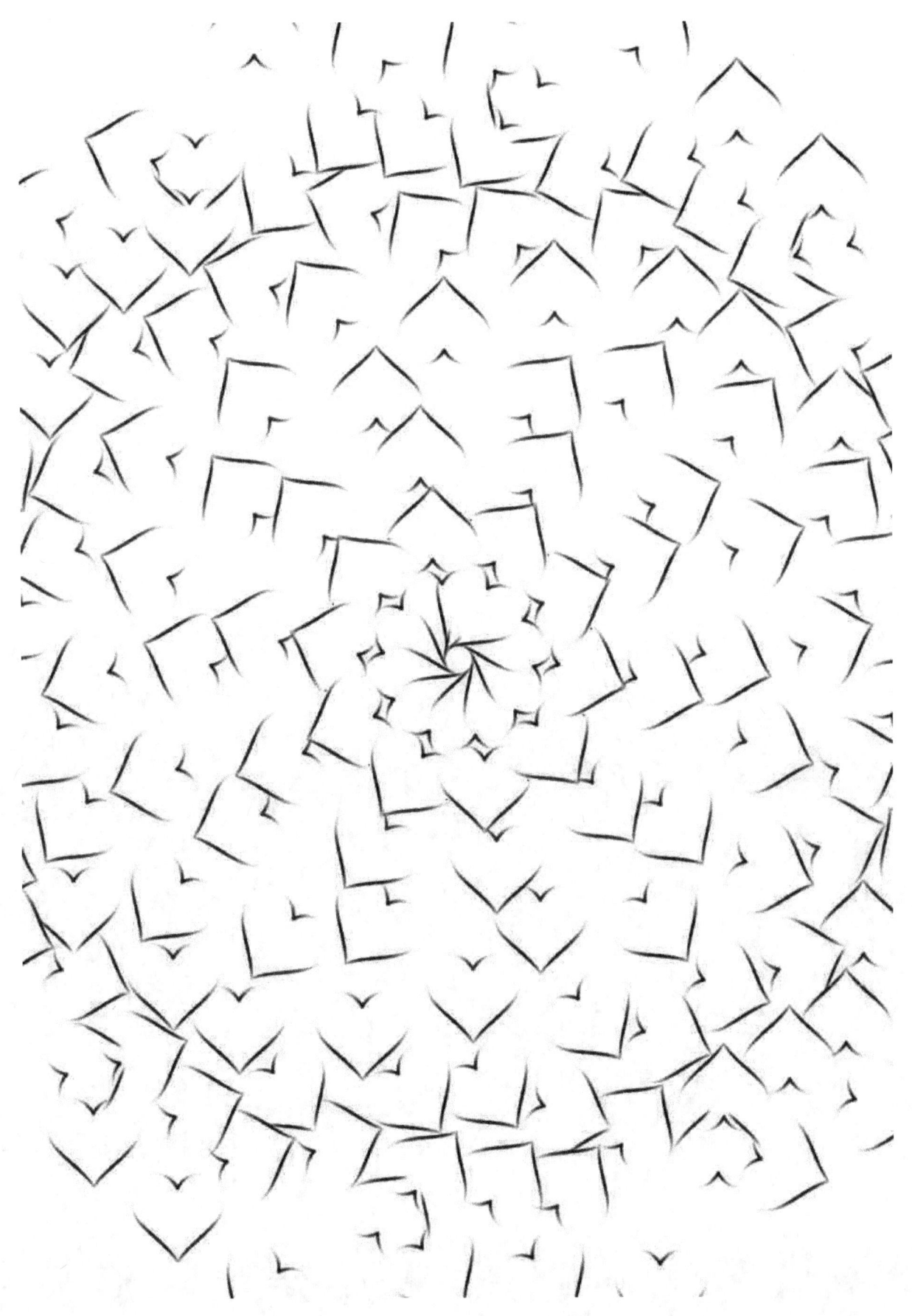

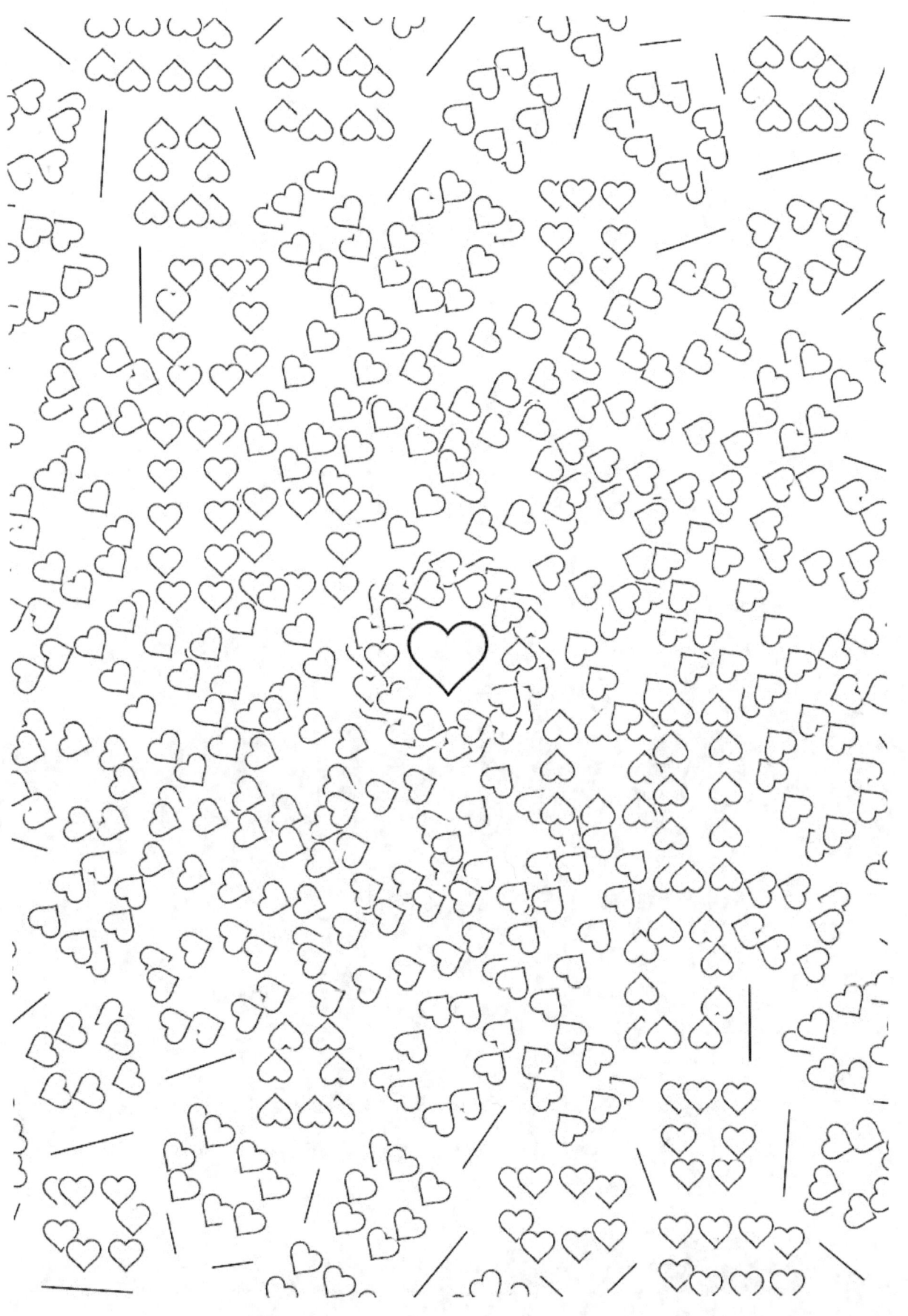

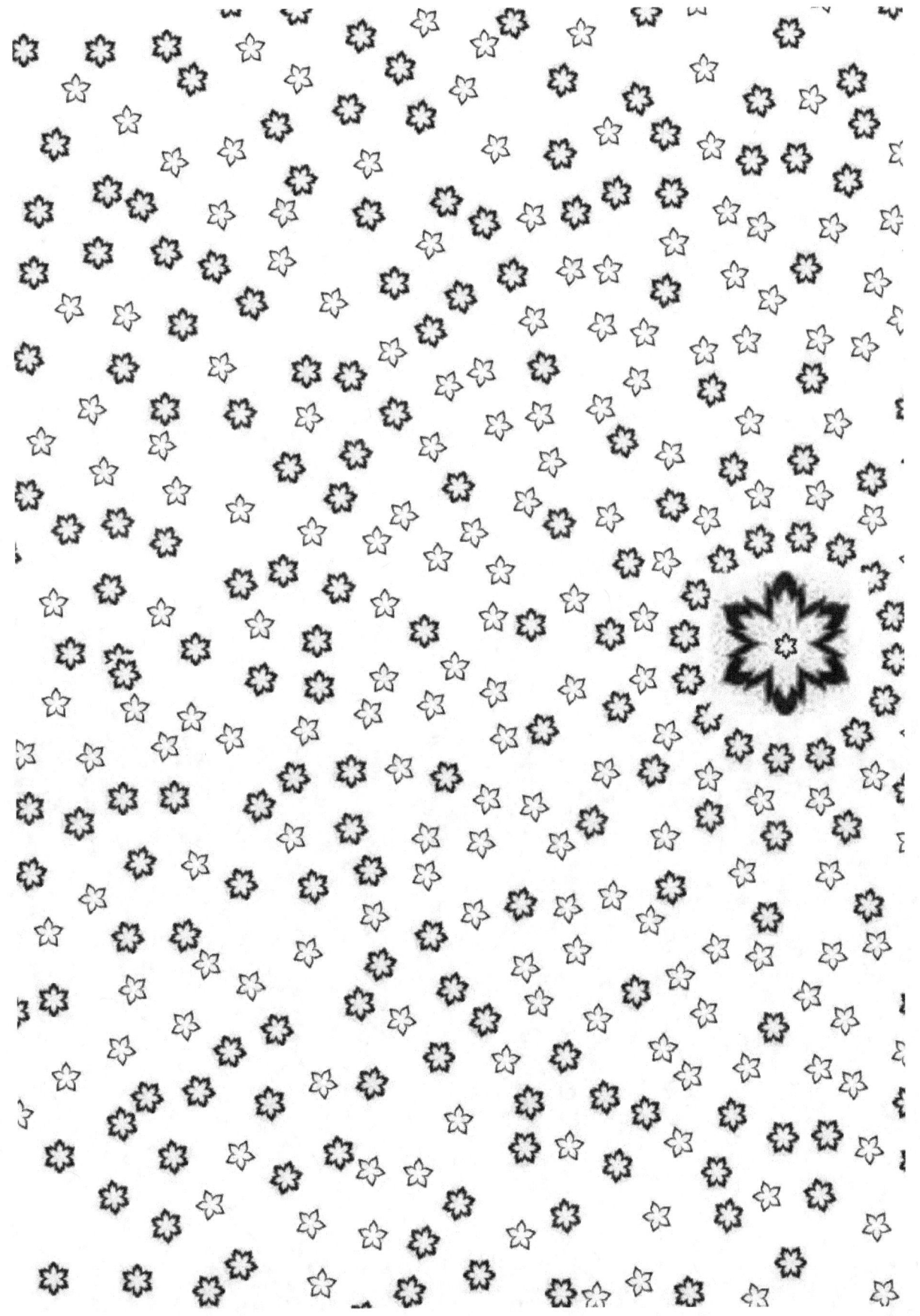

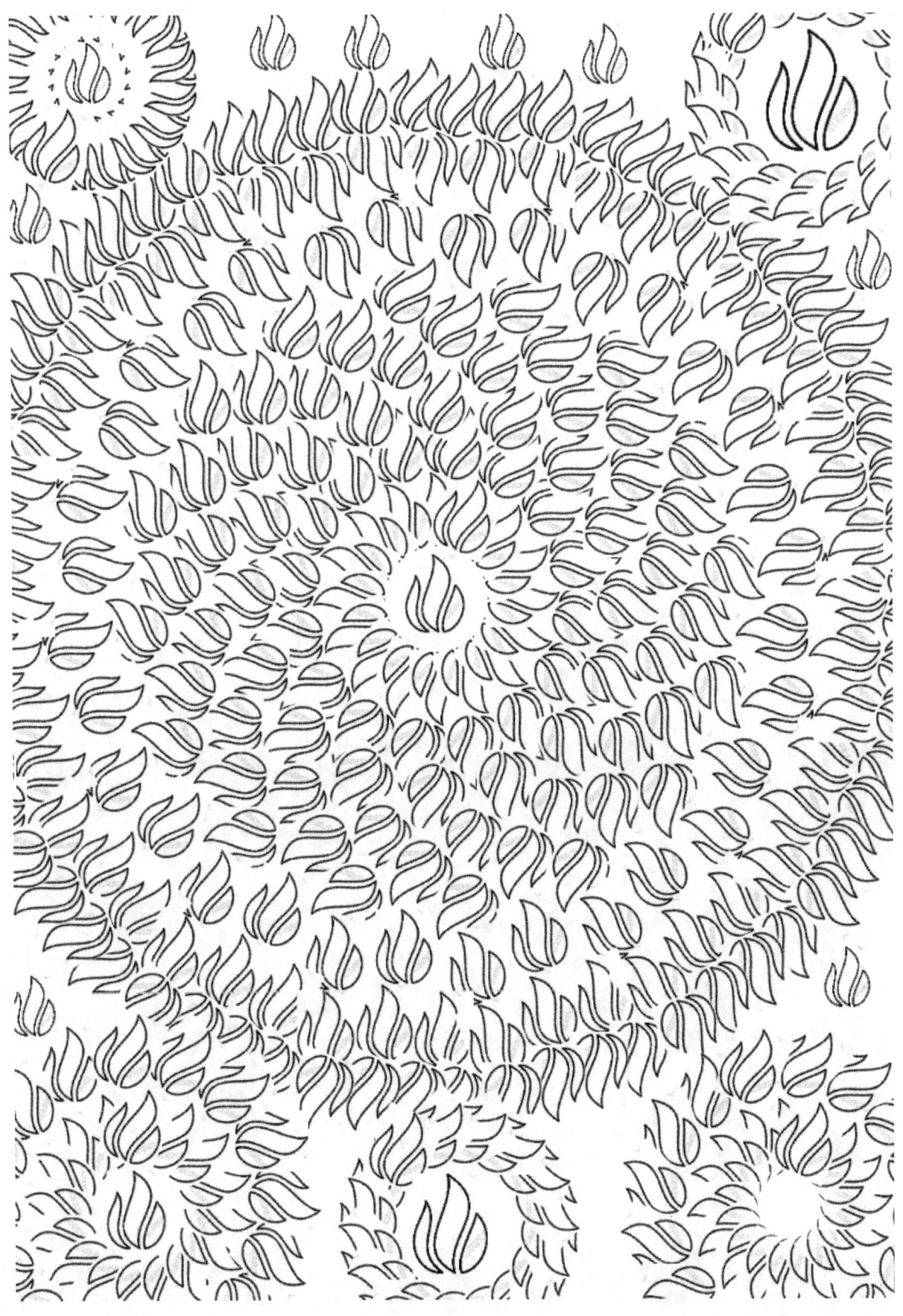

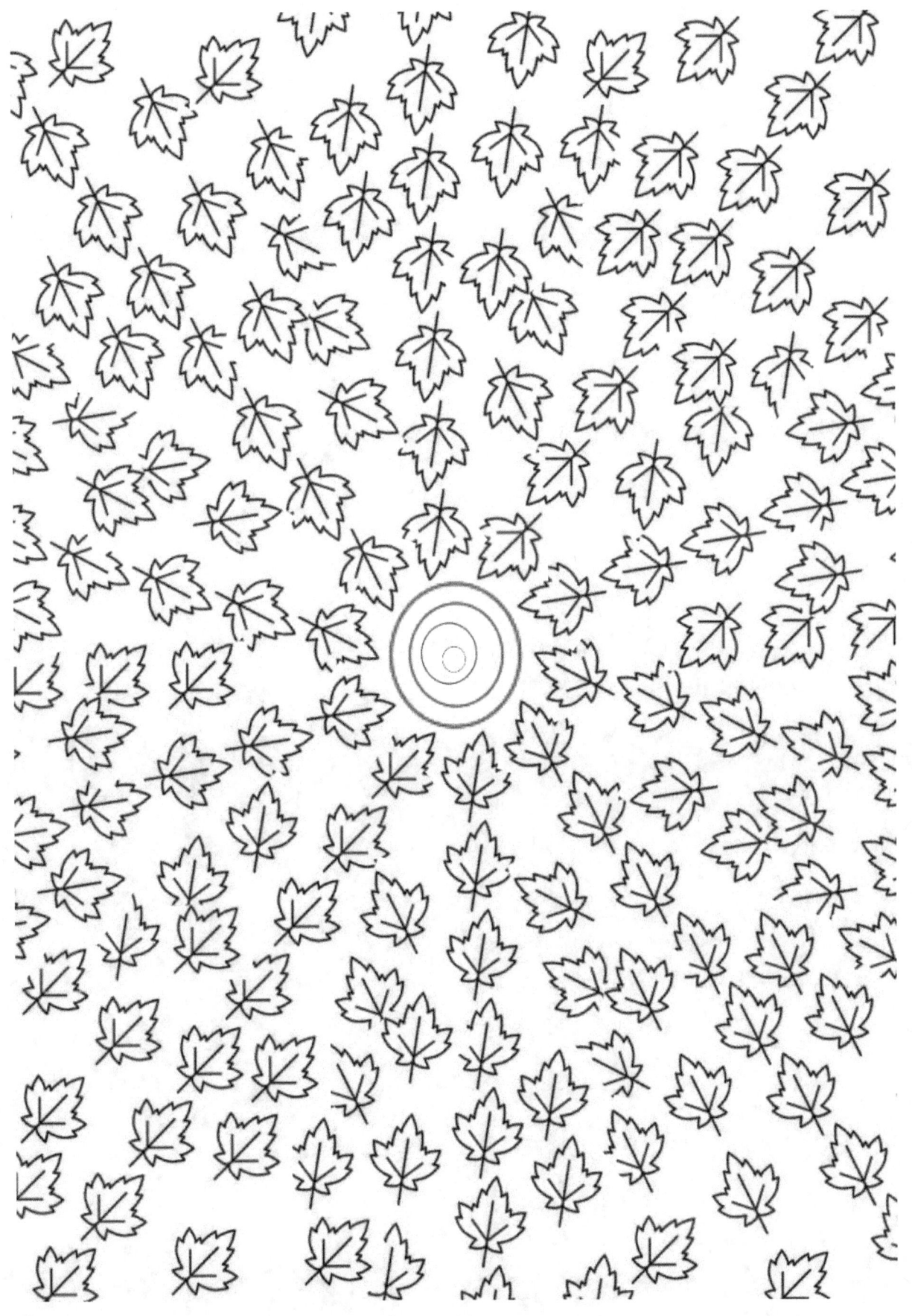

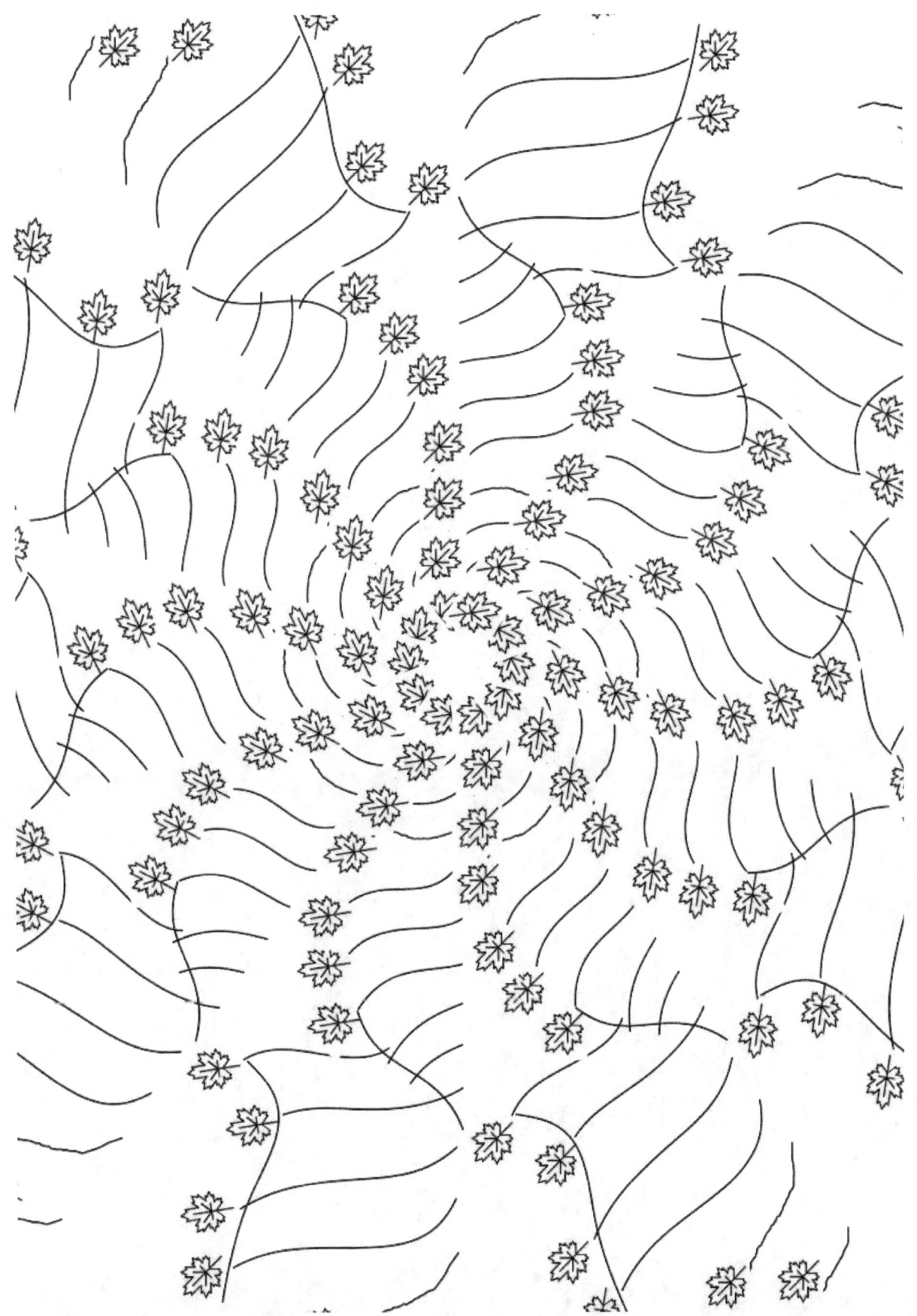

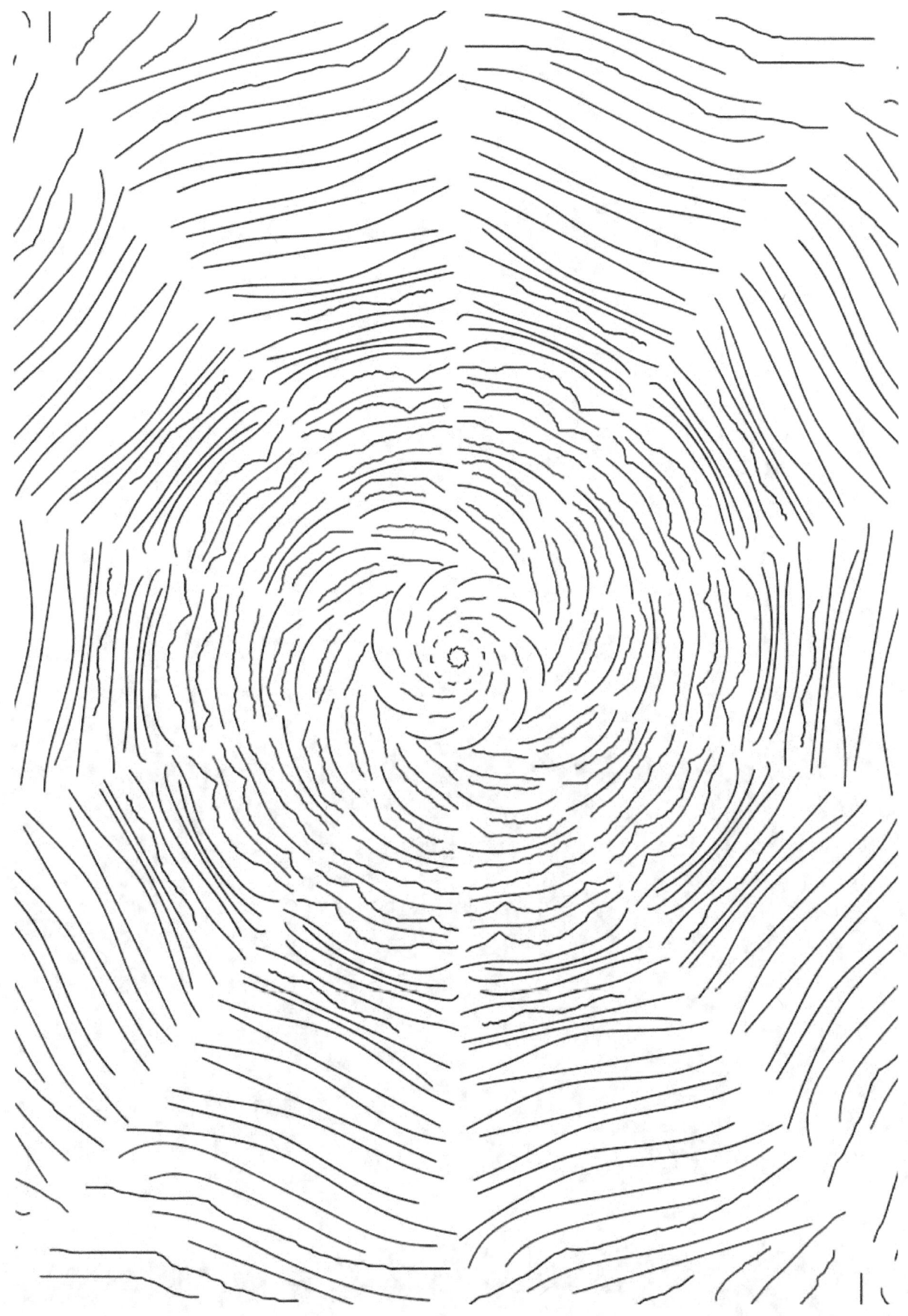

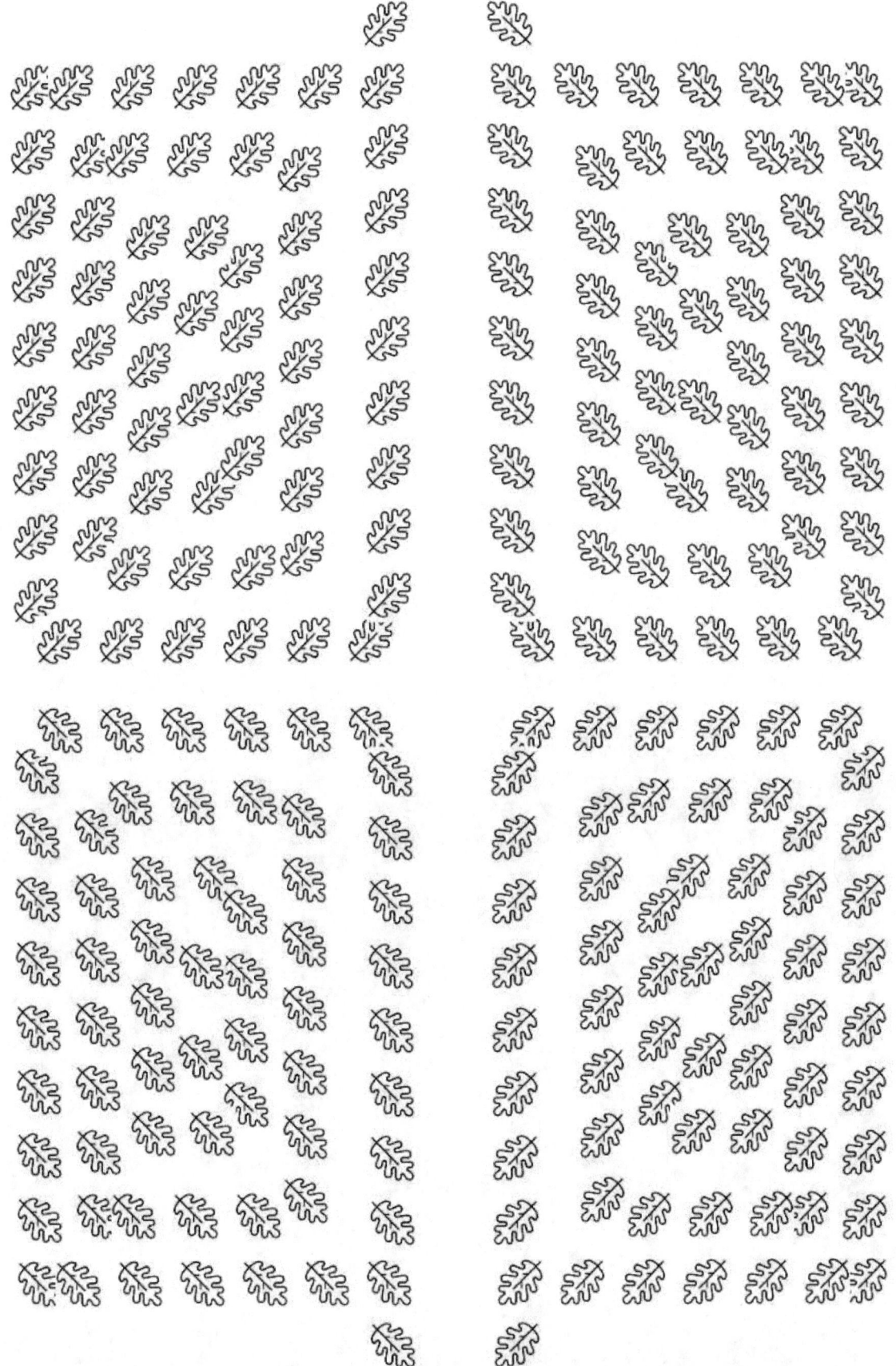

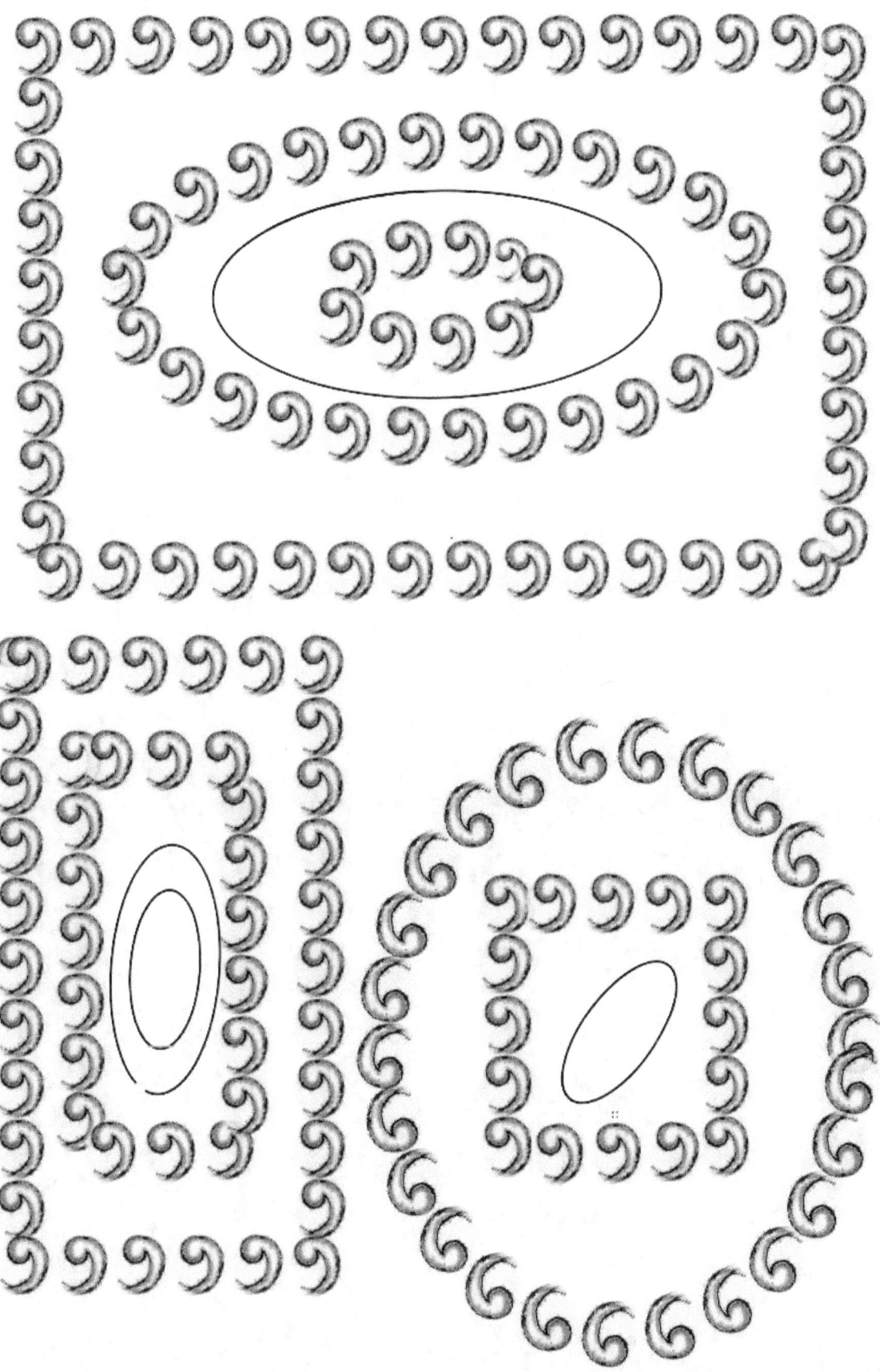

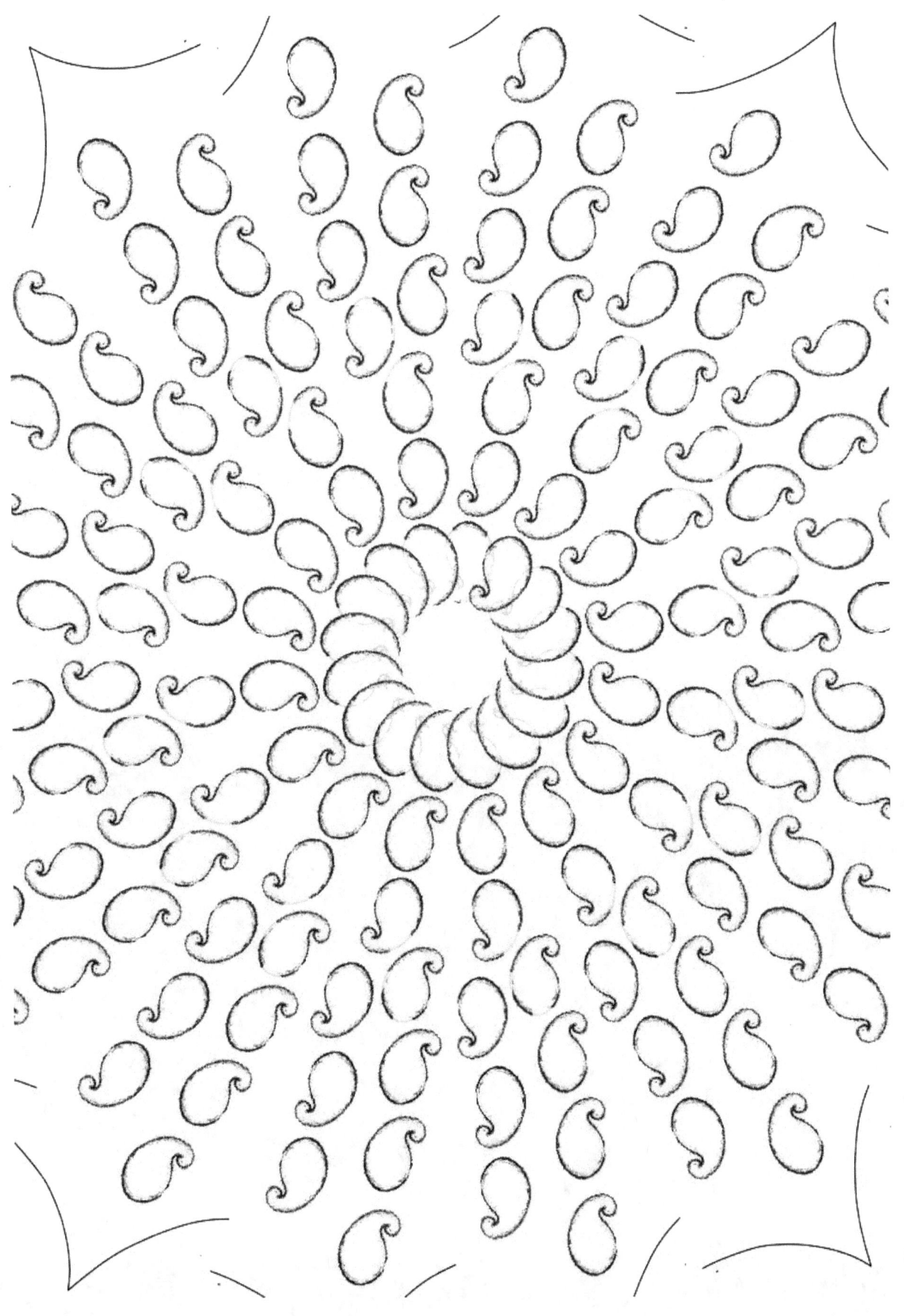

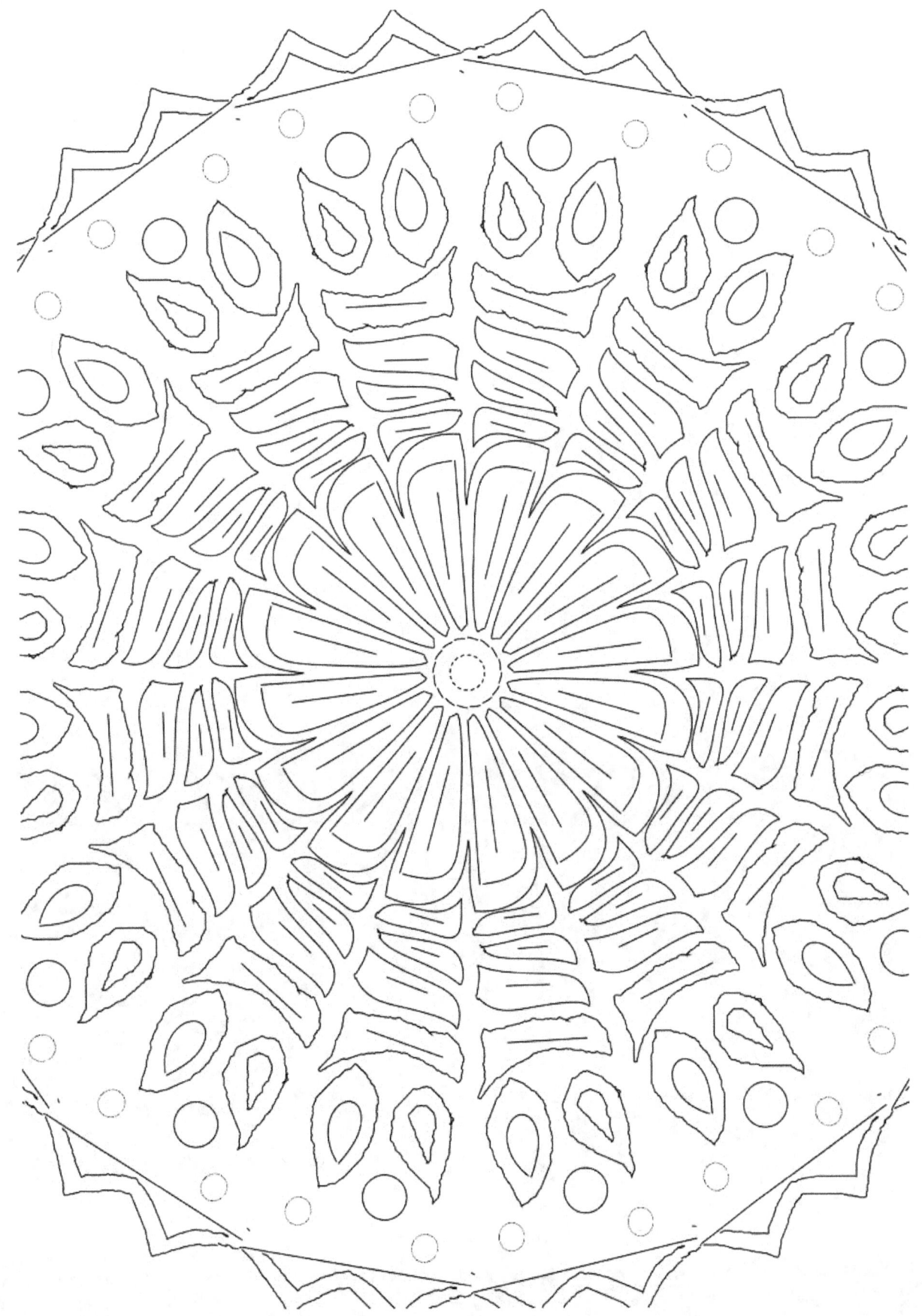

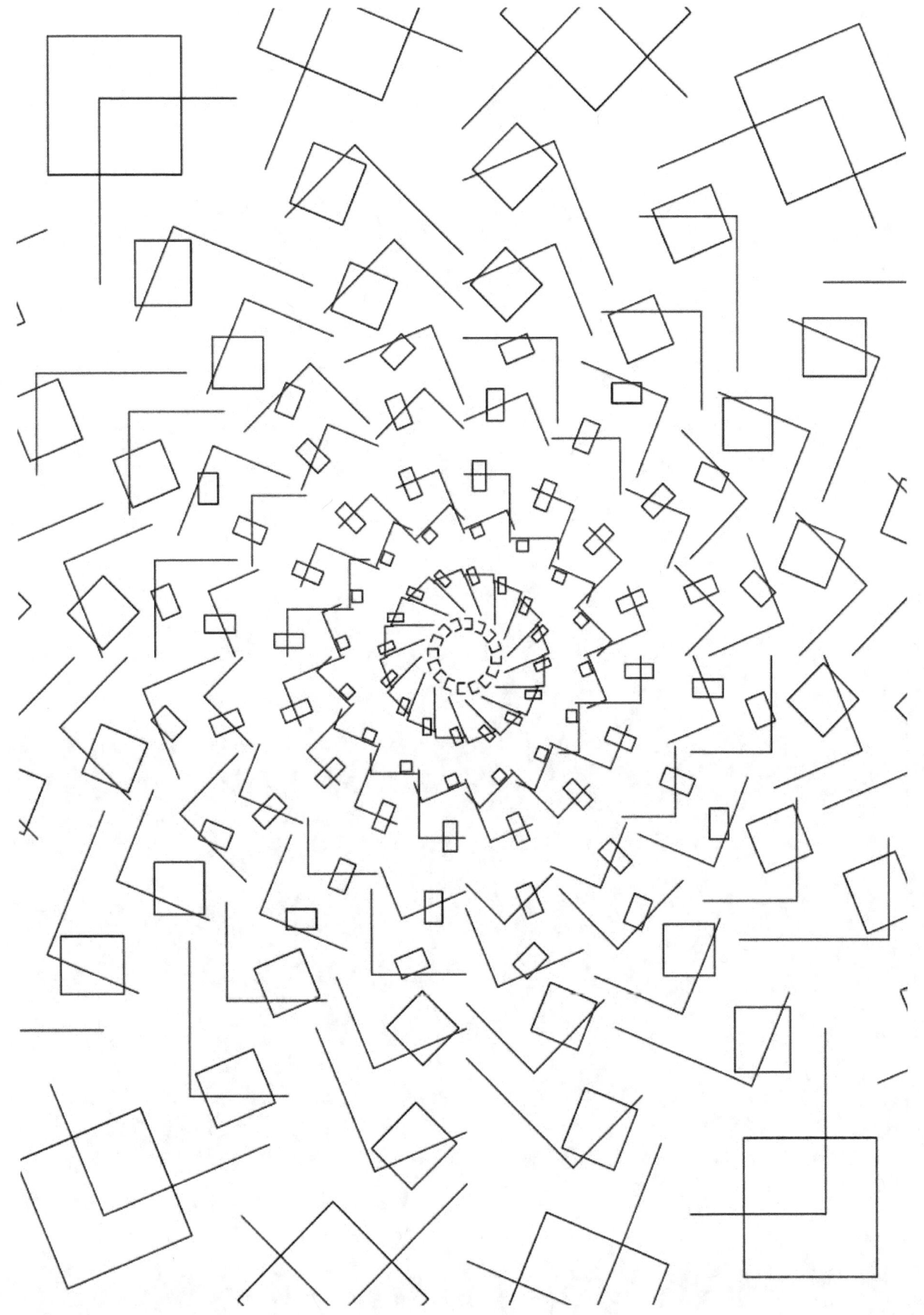

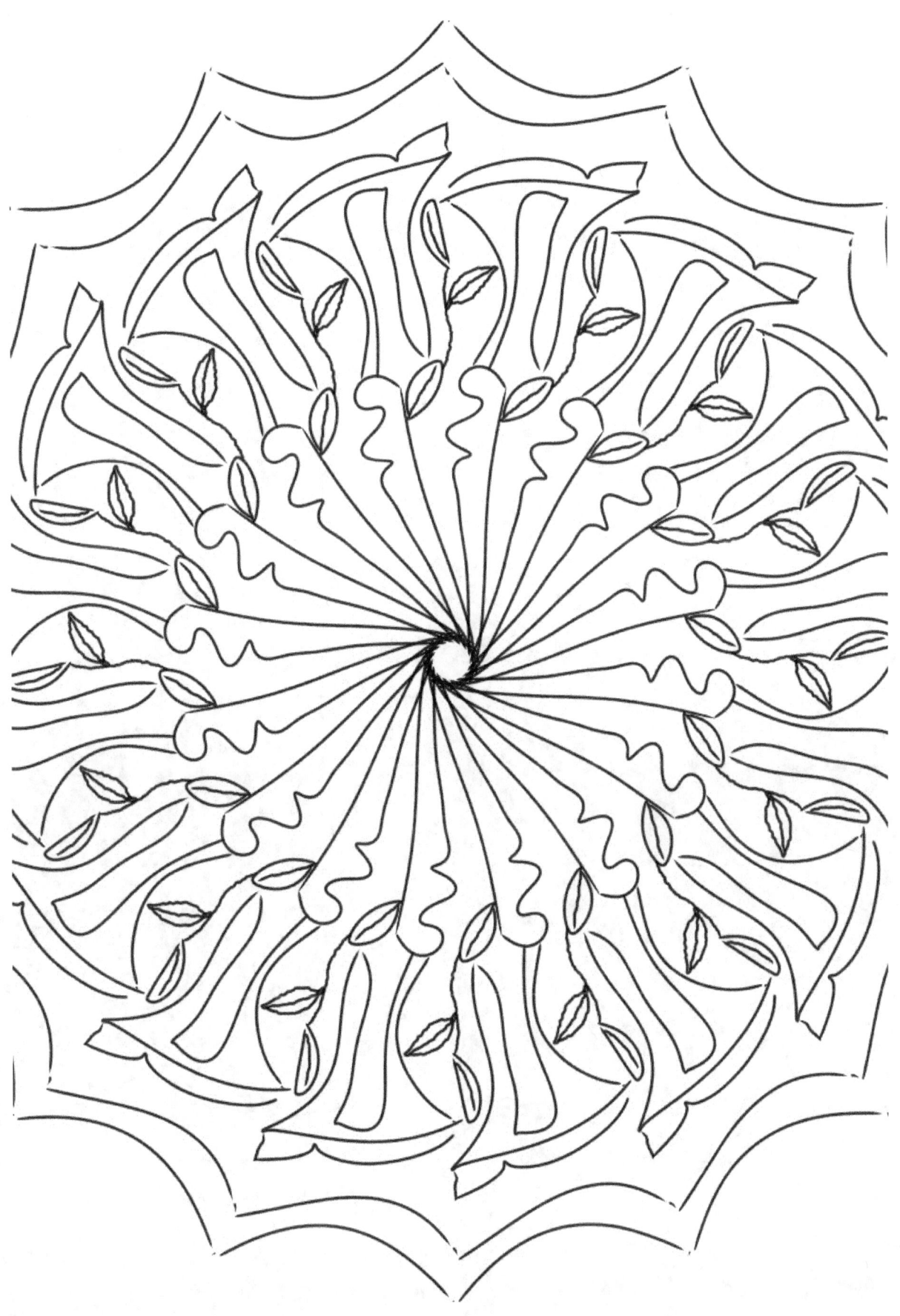

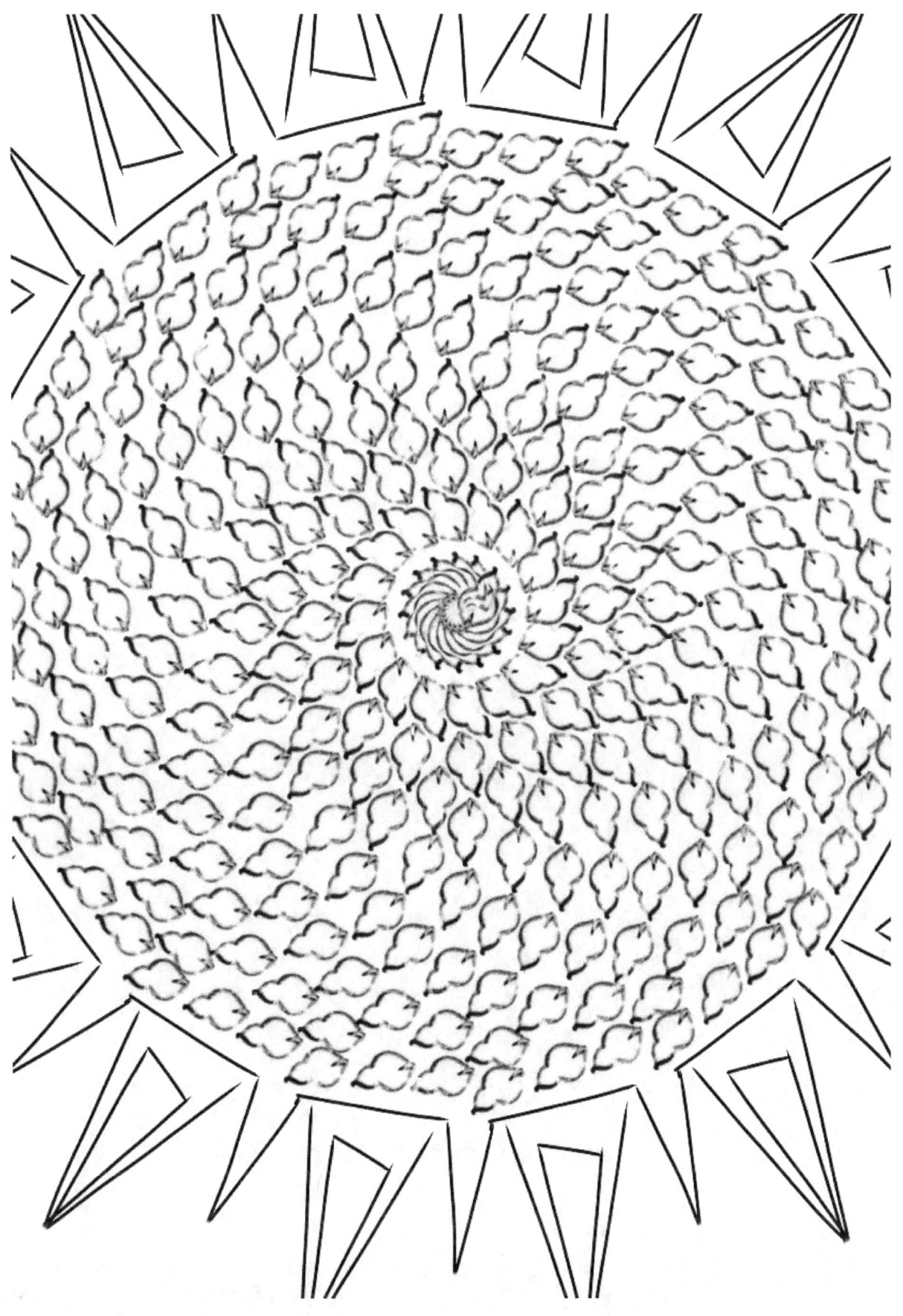

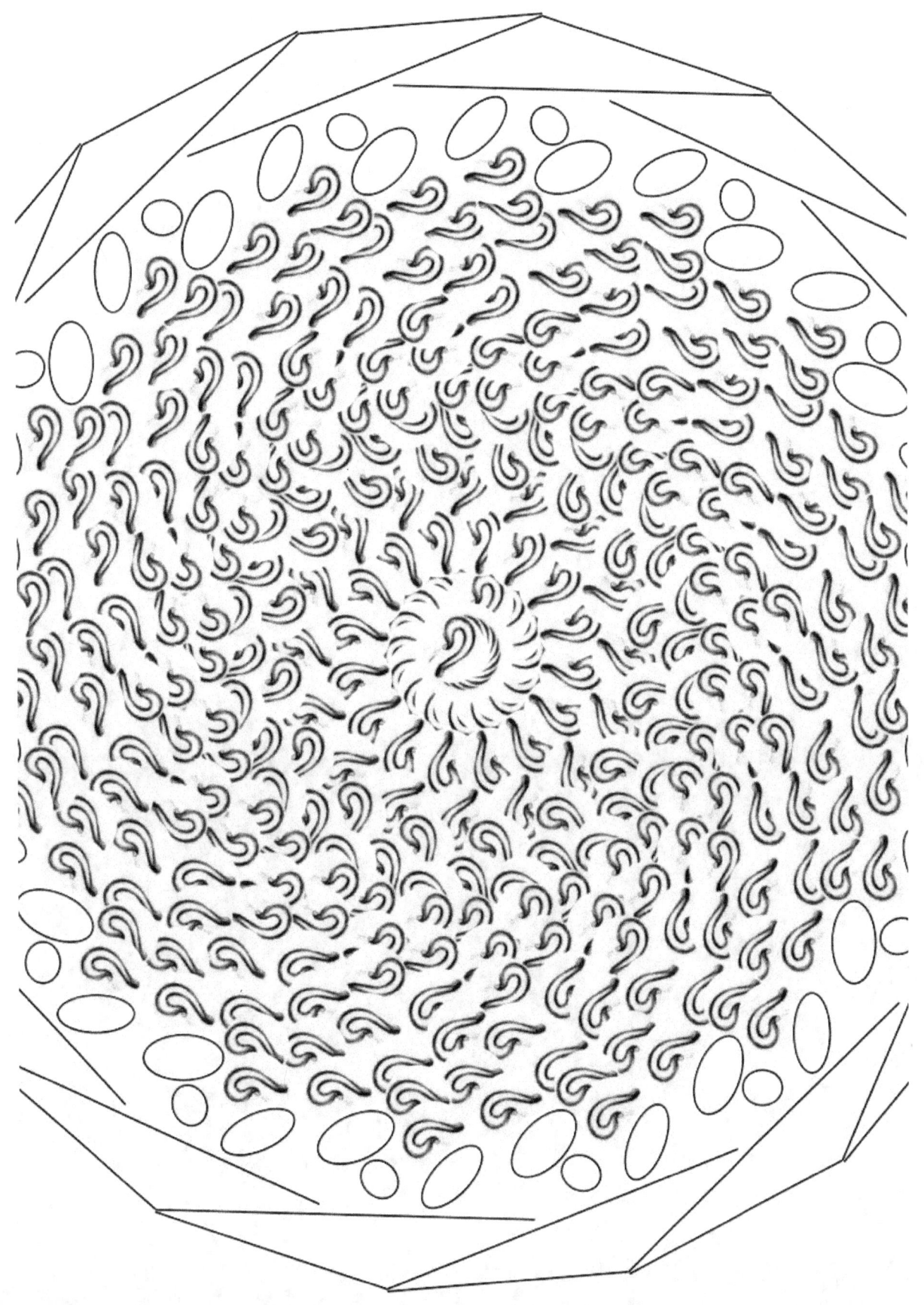

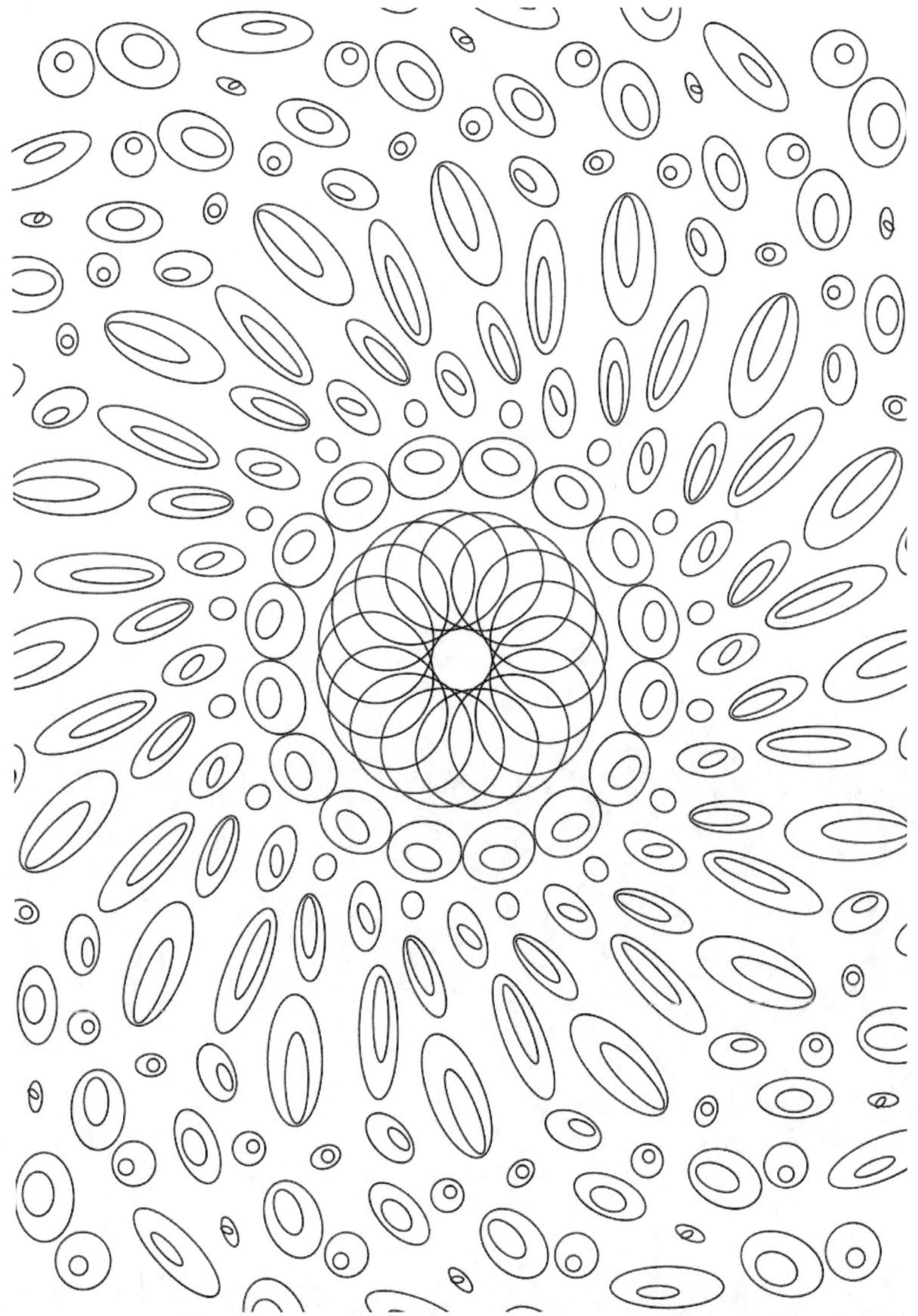

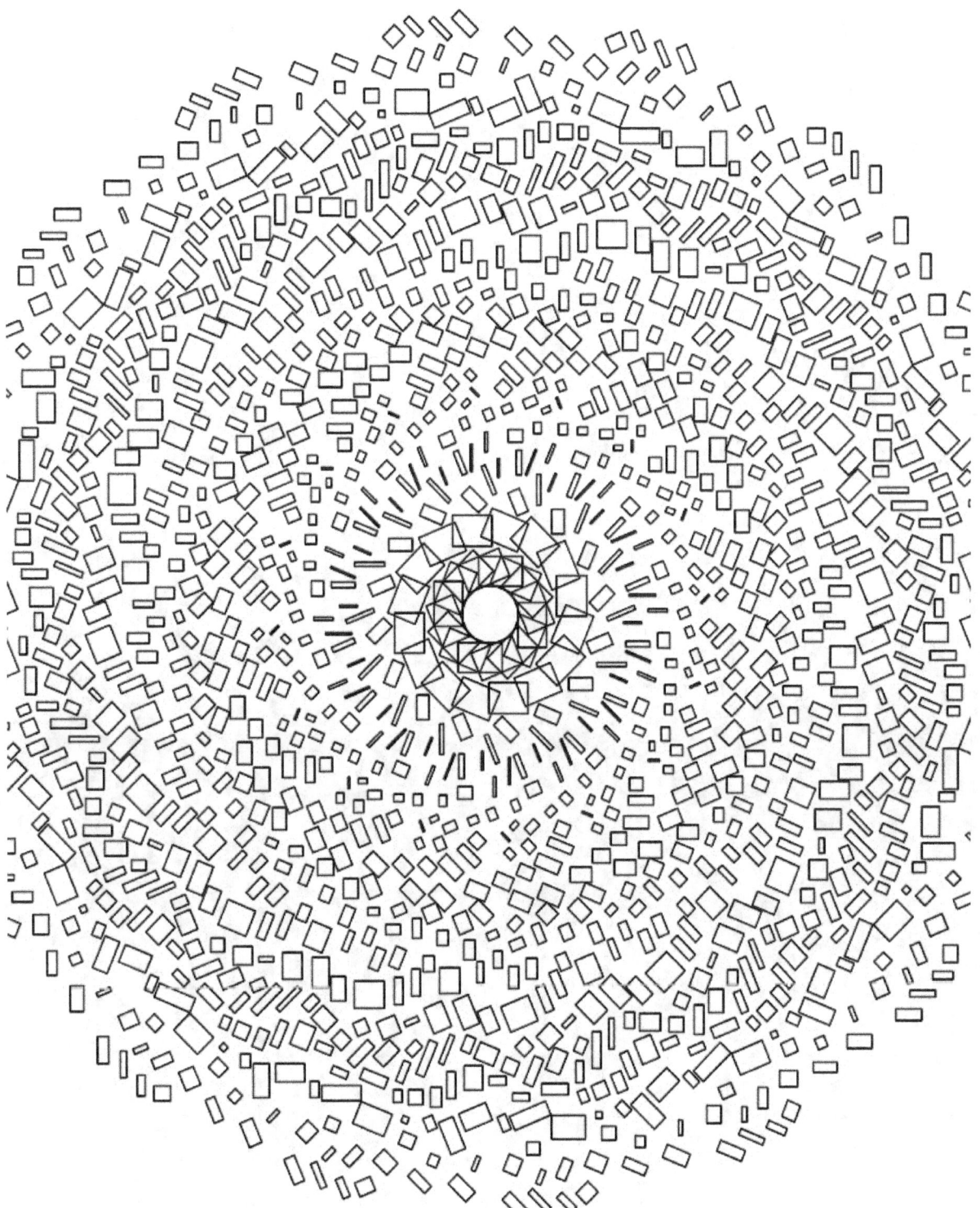

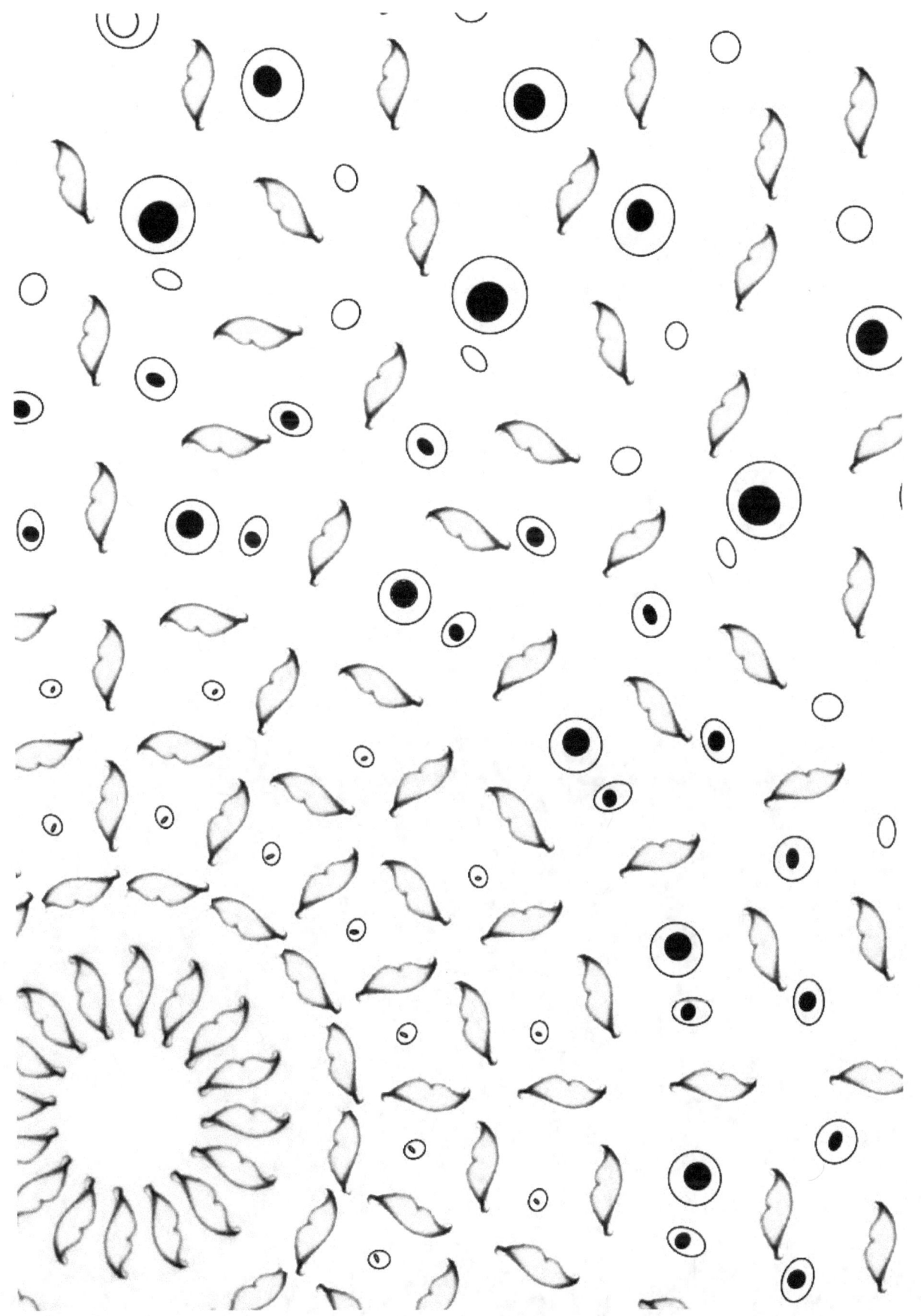

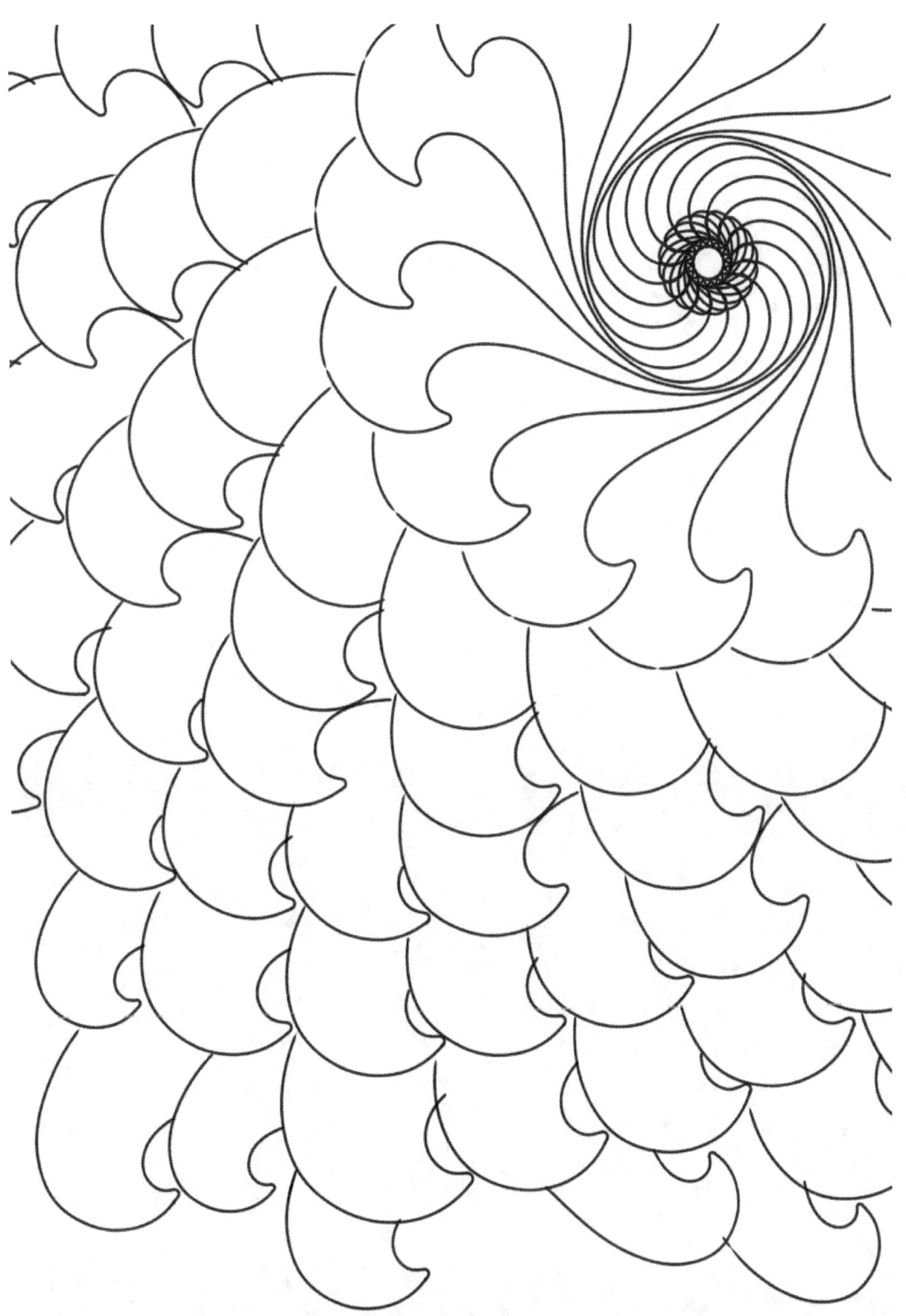

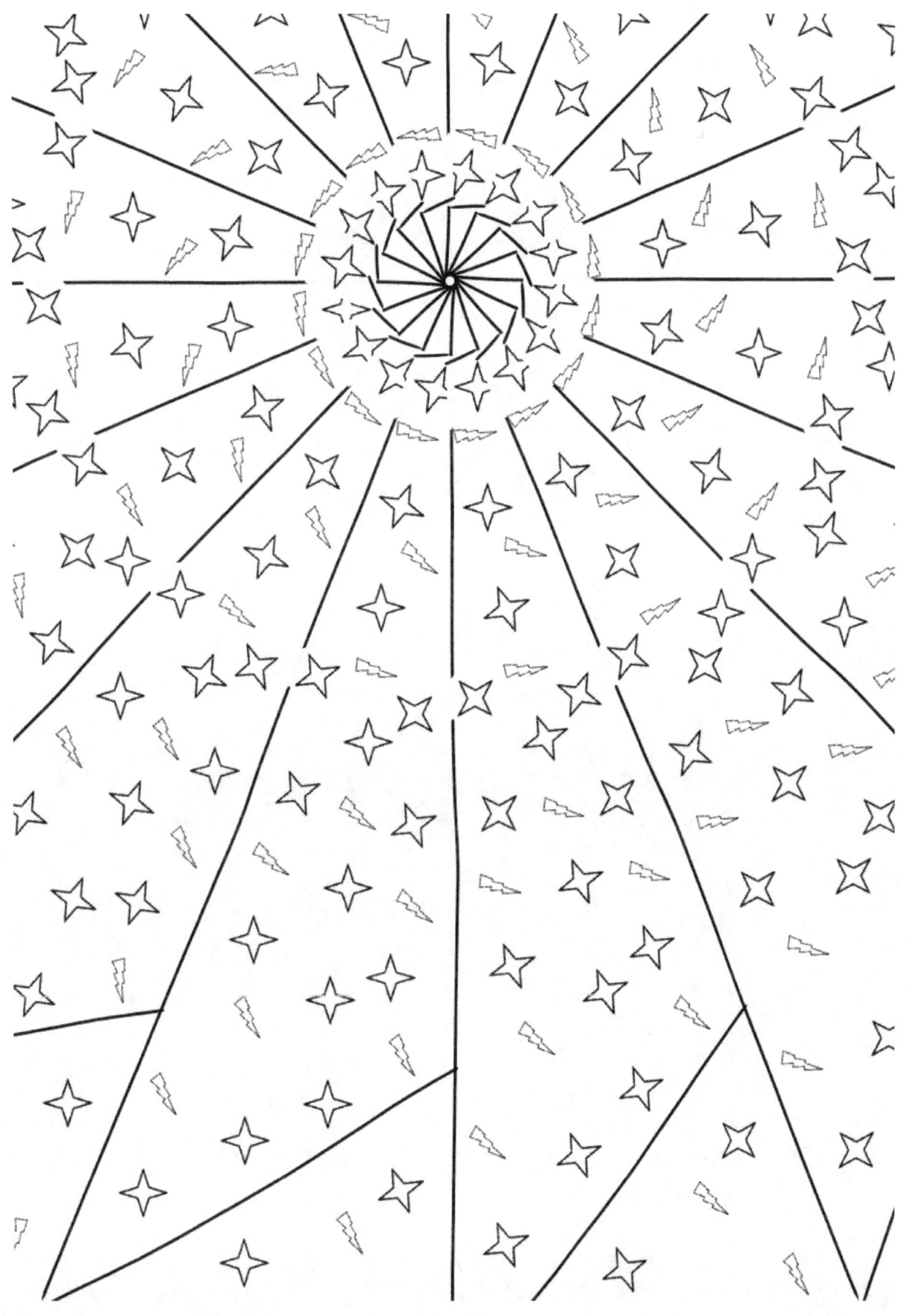

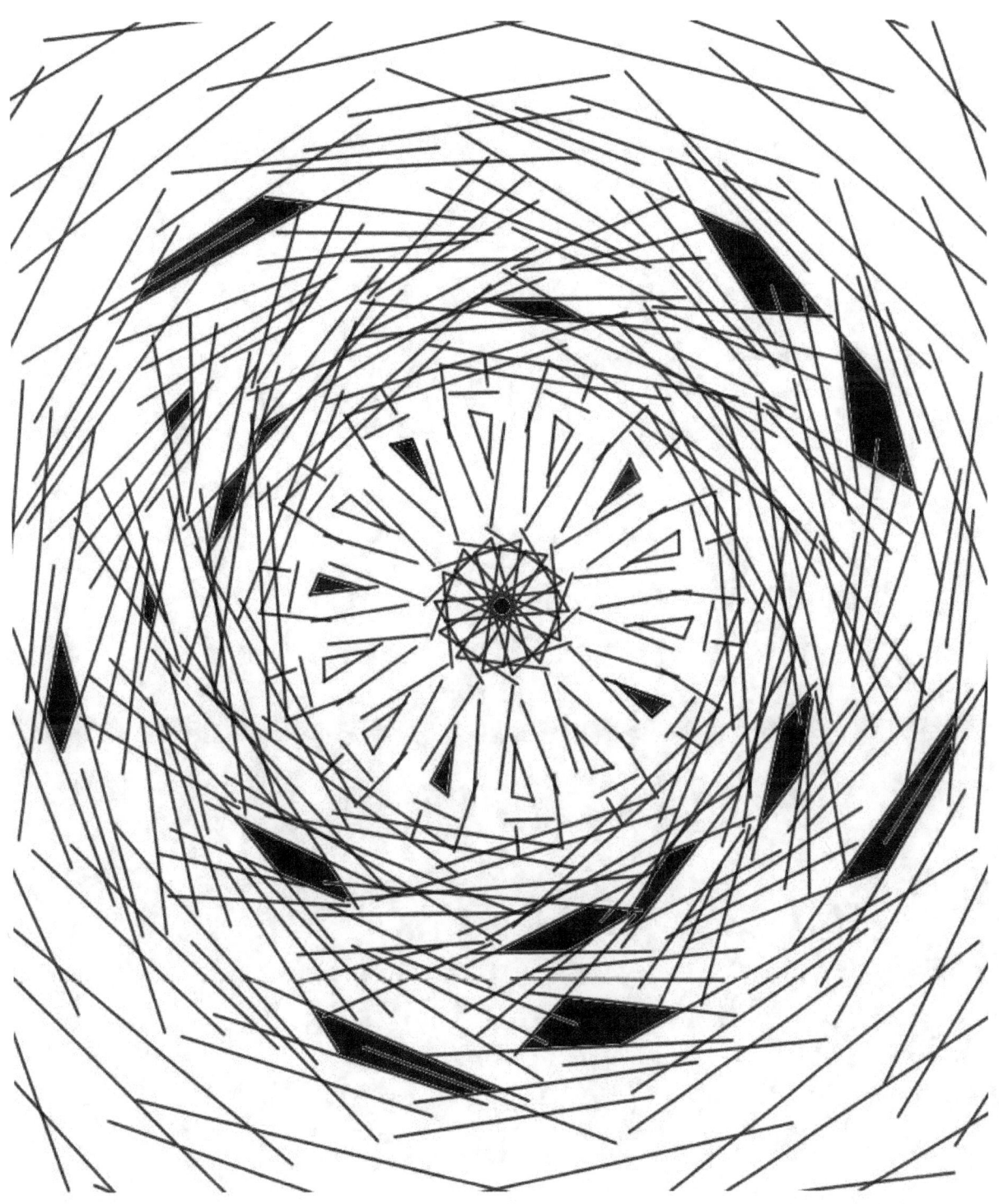

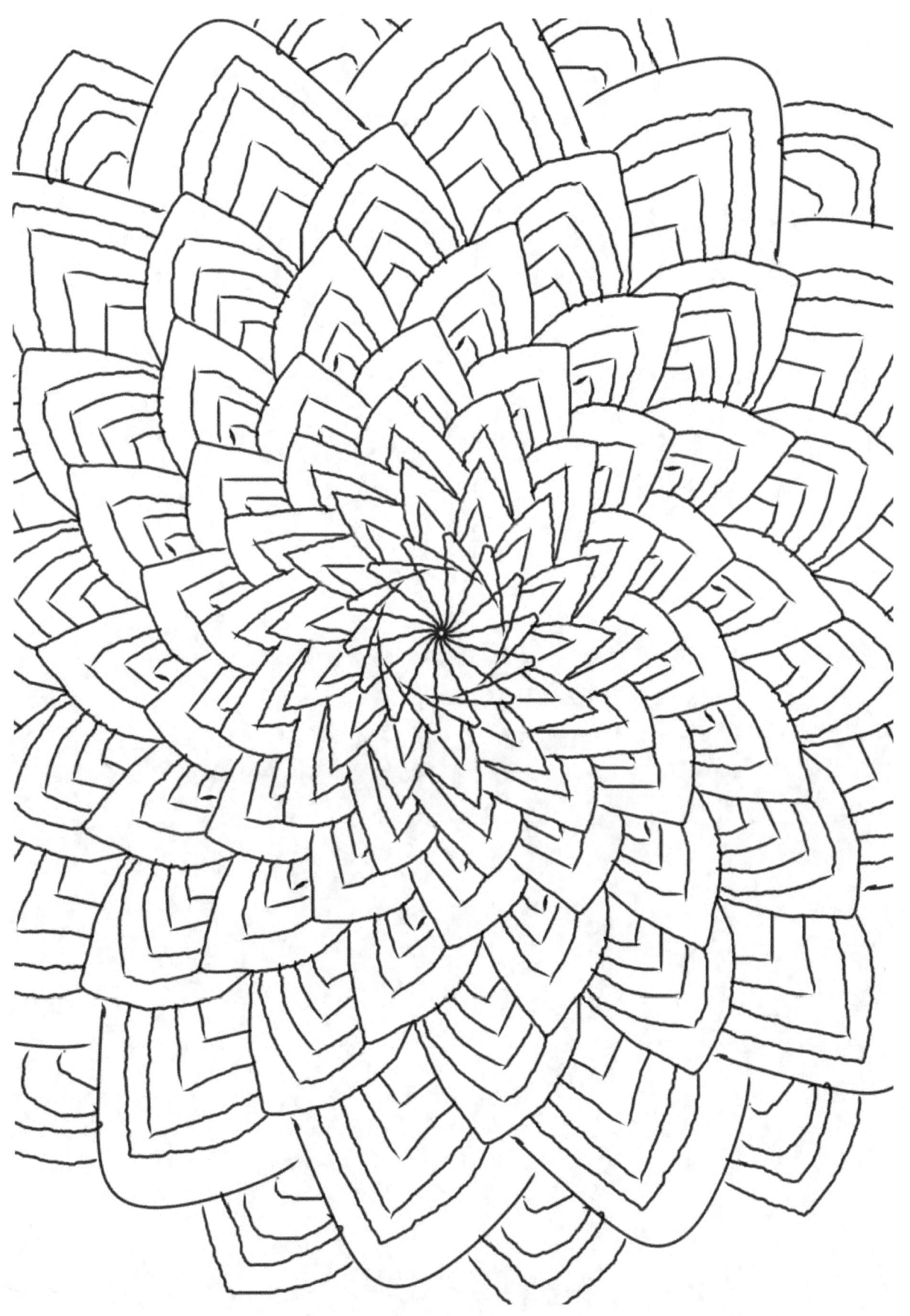

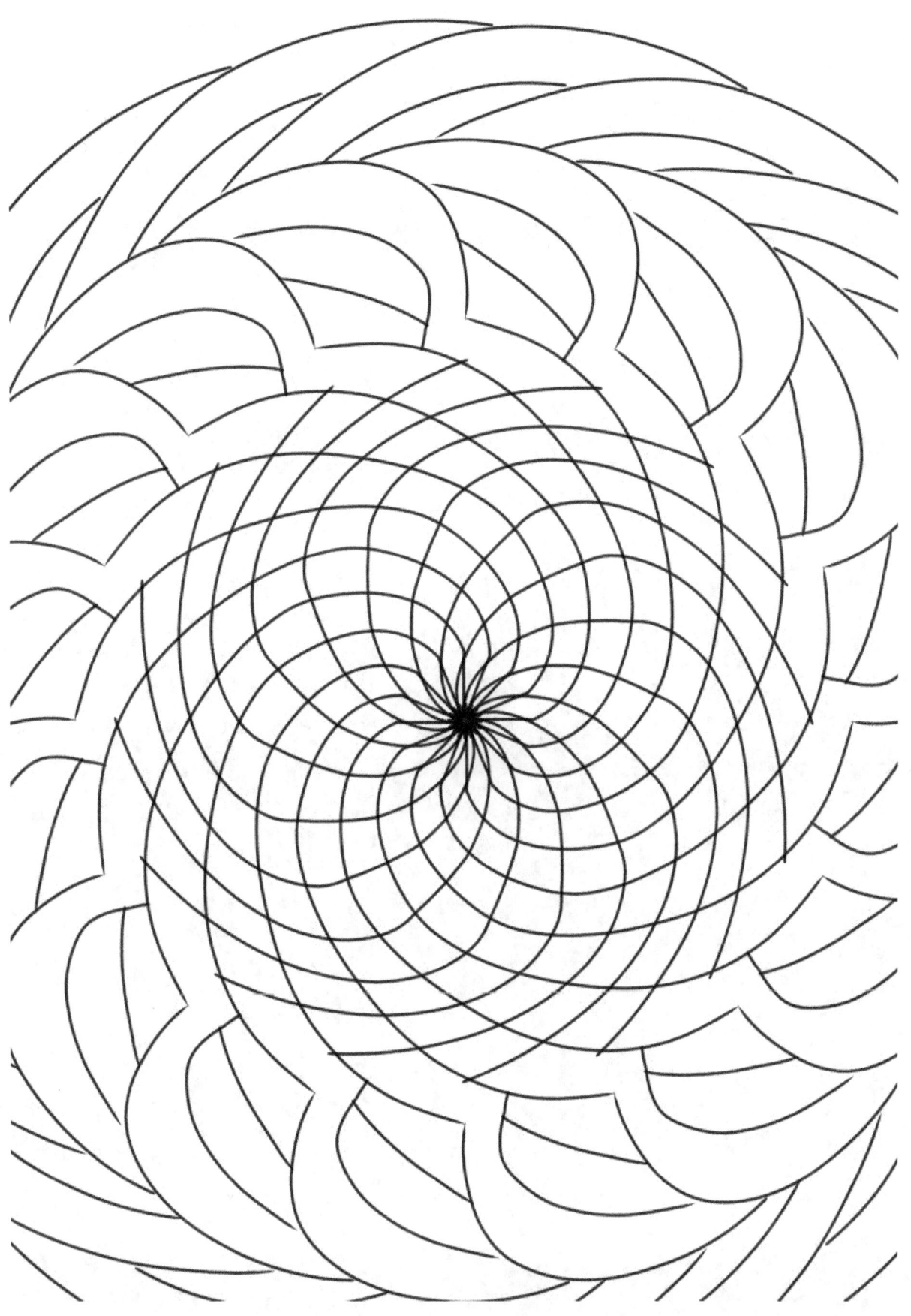

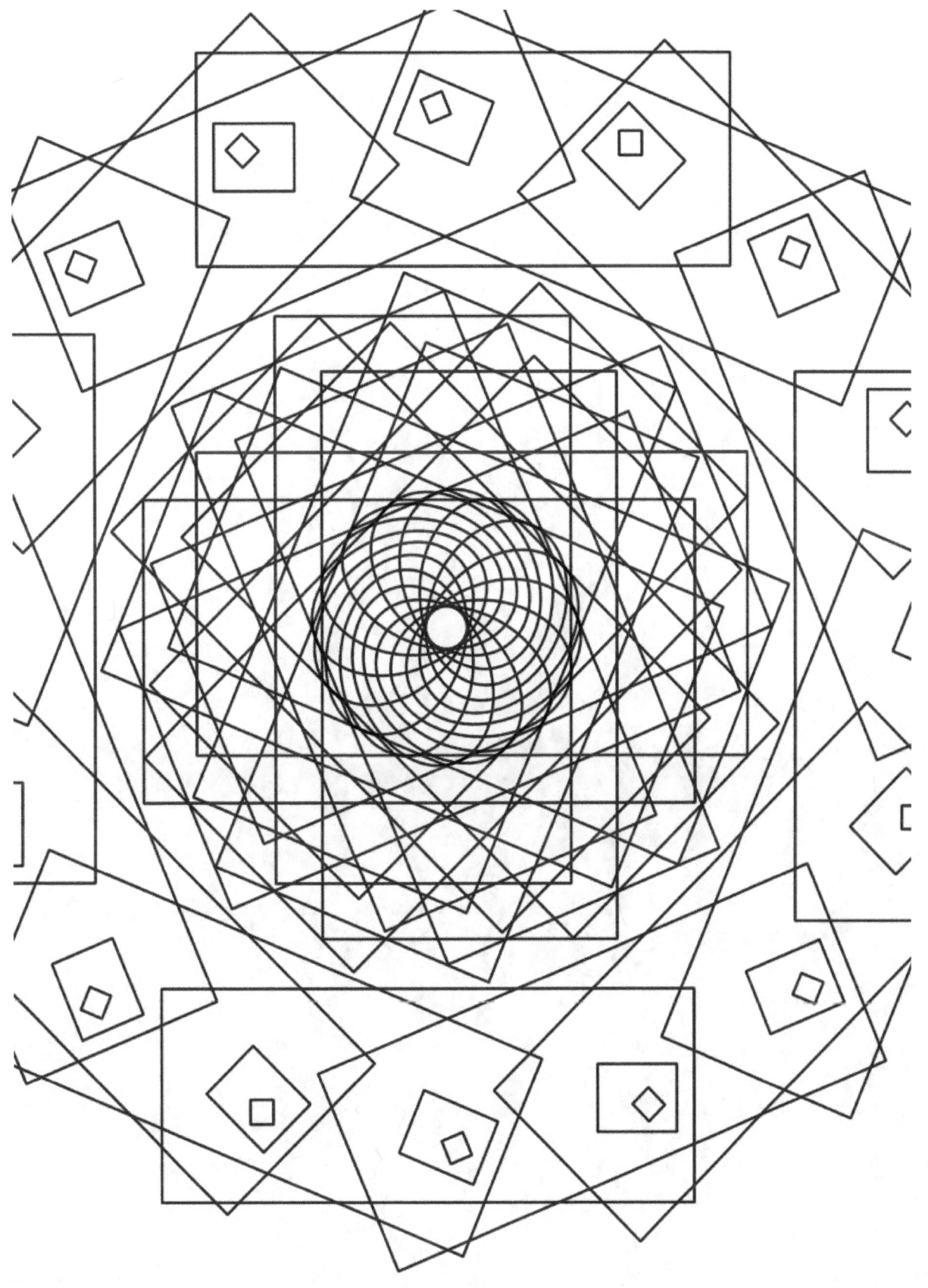

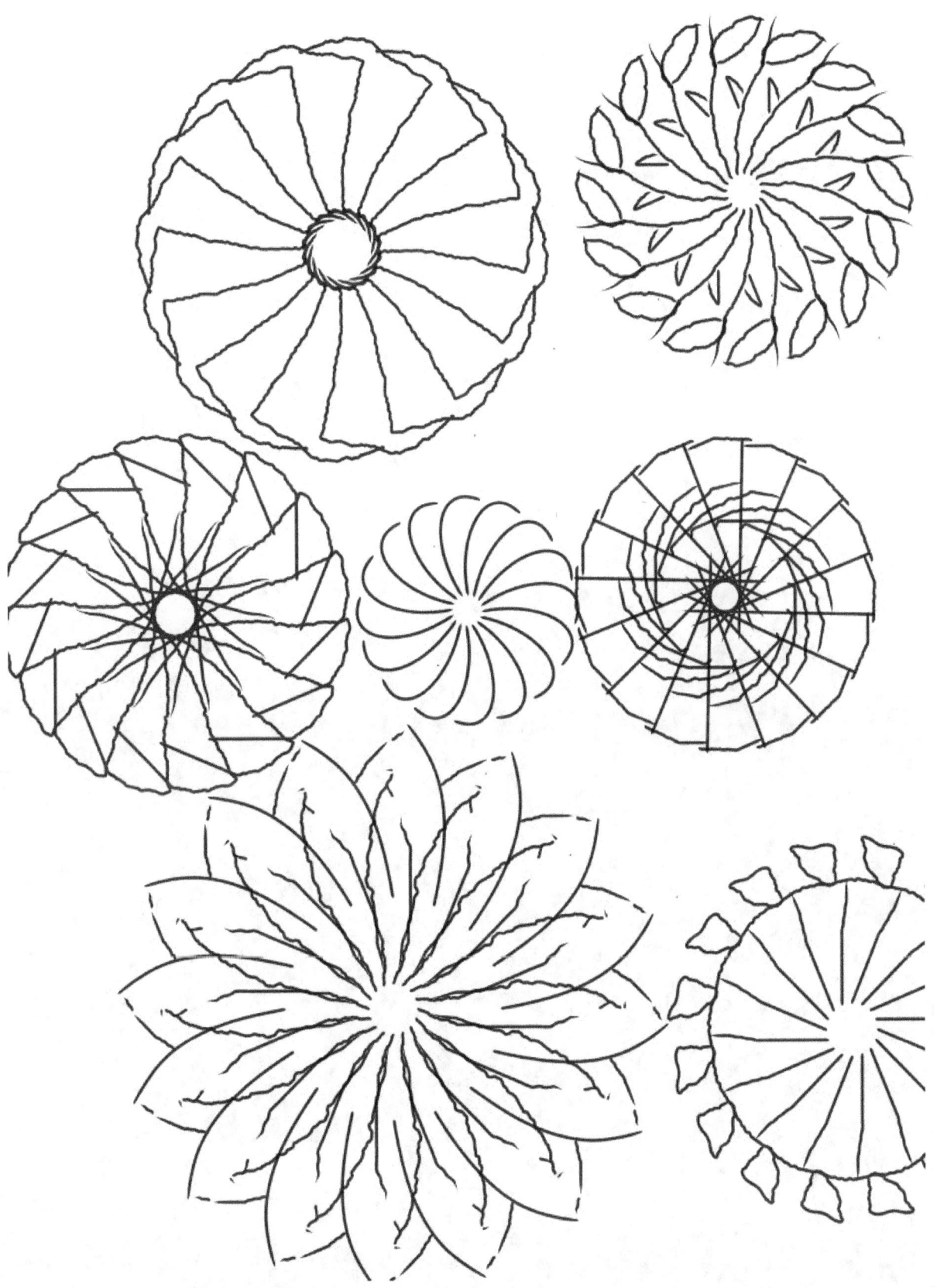

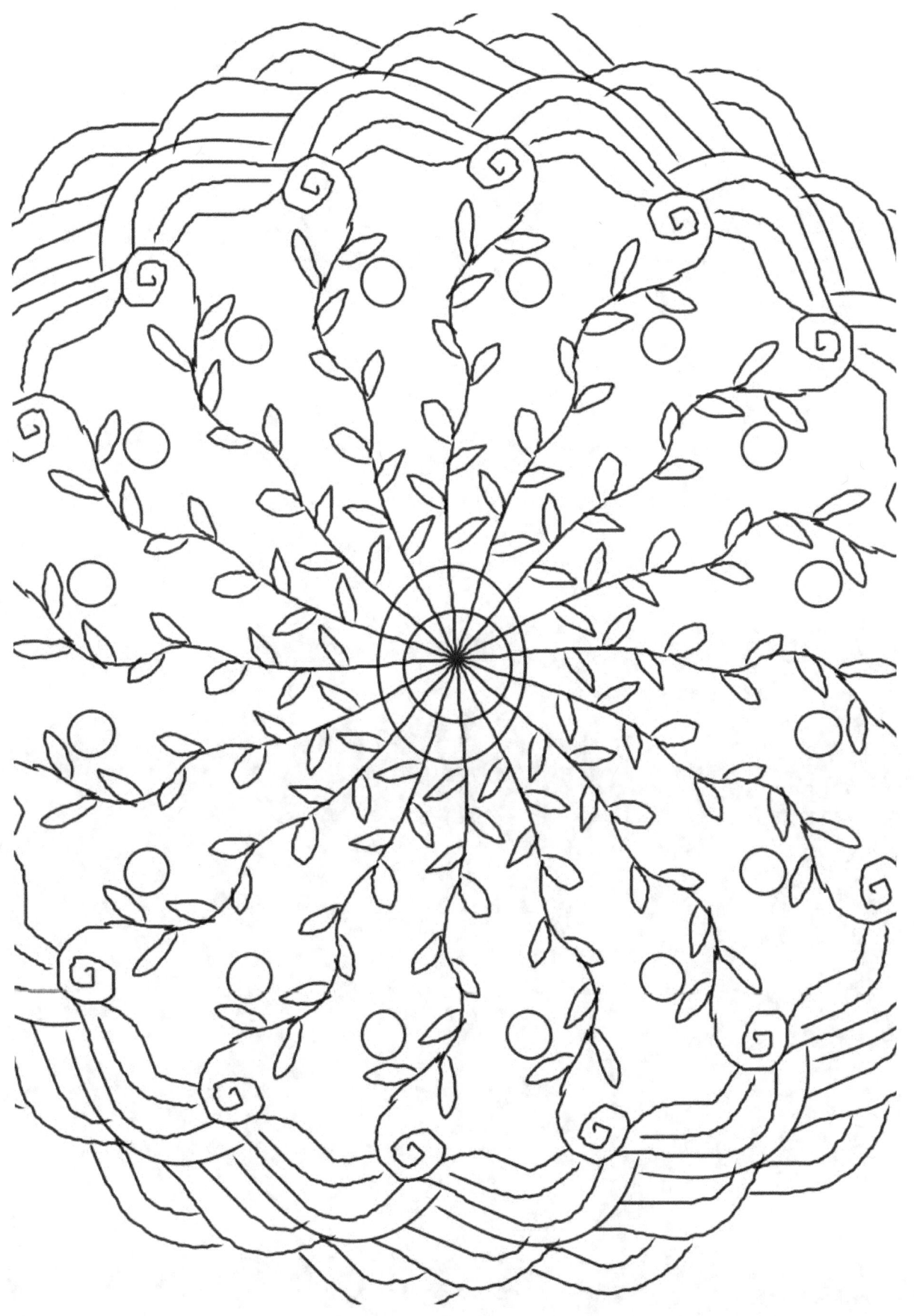

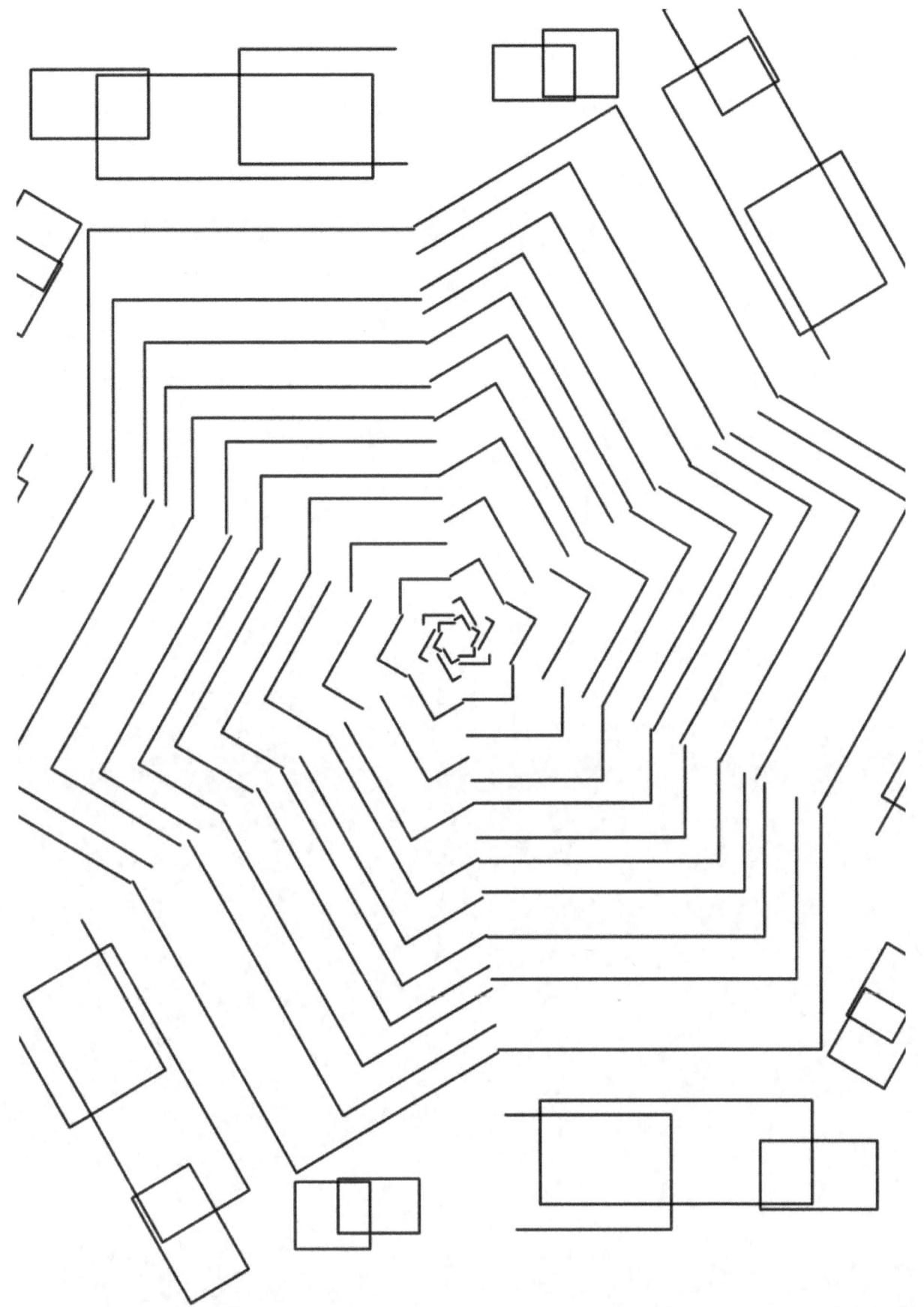

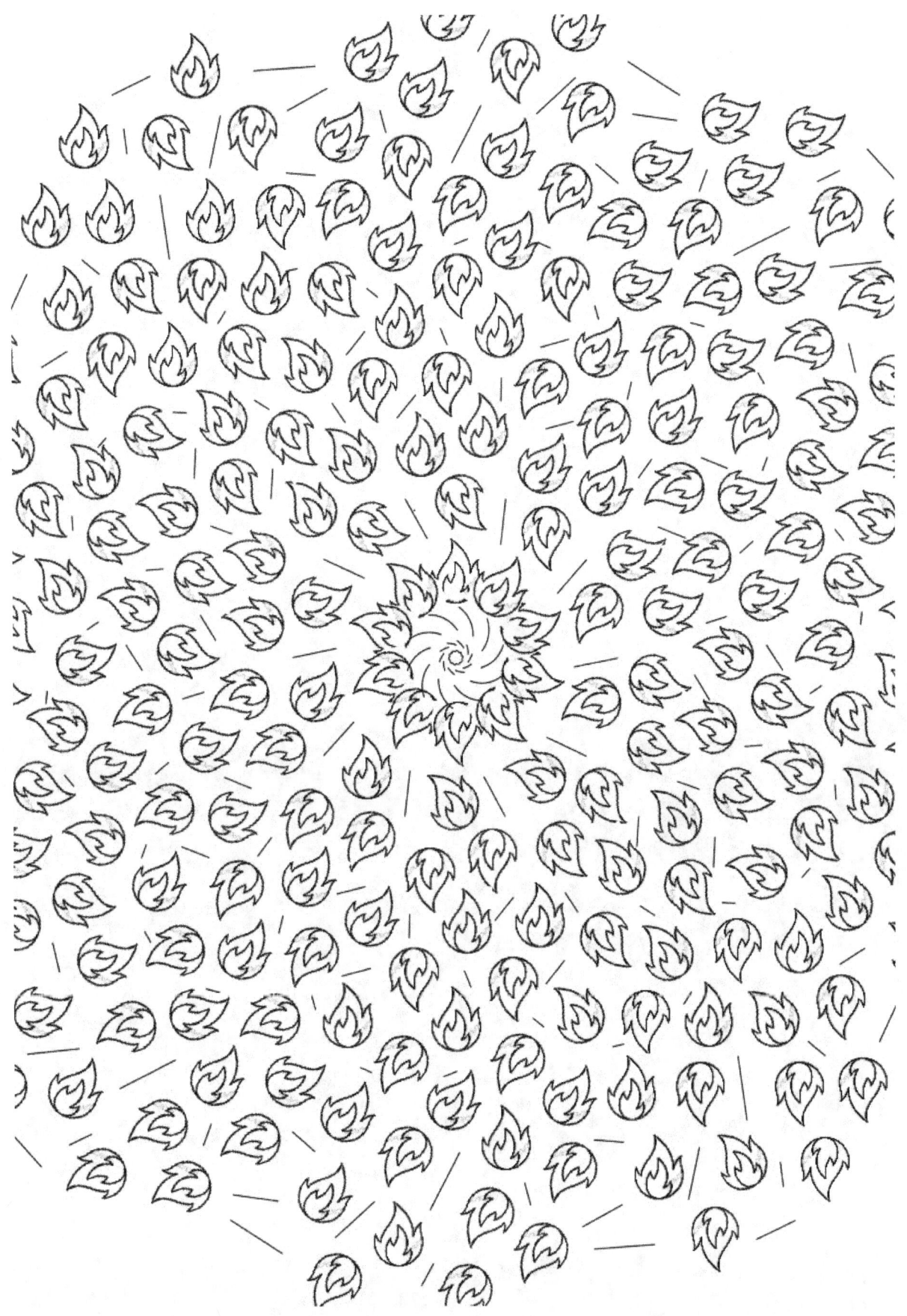

REQUEST TO READERS:

Dear Readers, please do me a favor,
Kindly provide feedback by giving a genuine review about this book
on the amazon page. This will help us provide more such books.
This will also promote this book so that more and more readers like
and appreciate this book. Your opinions will have a great deal of
impact on further books of this series and help us understand the kind
of work you would like to see as a reader.

You can also provide more inform on my contact information such as
my email personally. All suggestions are welcome.

A heartfelt thank you to all the readers of this book

AUTHOR DETAILS
Irfana Designs

Contact Information
Email: irfanadesigns@gmail.com

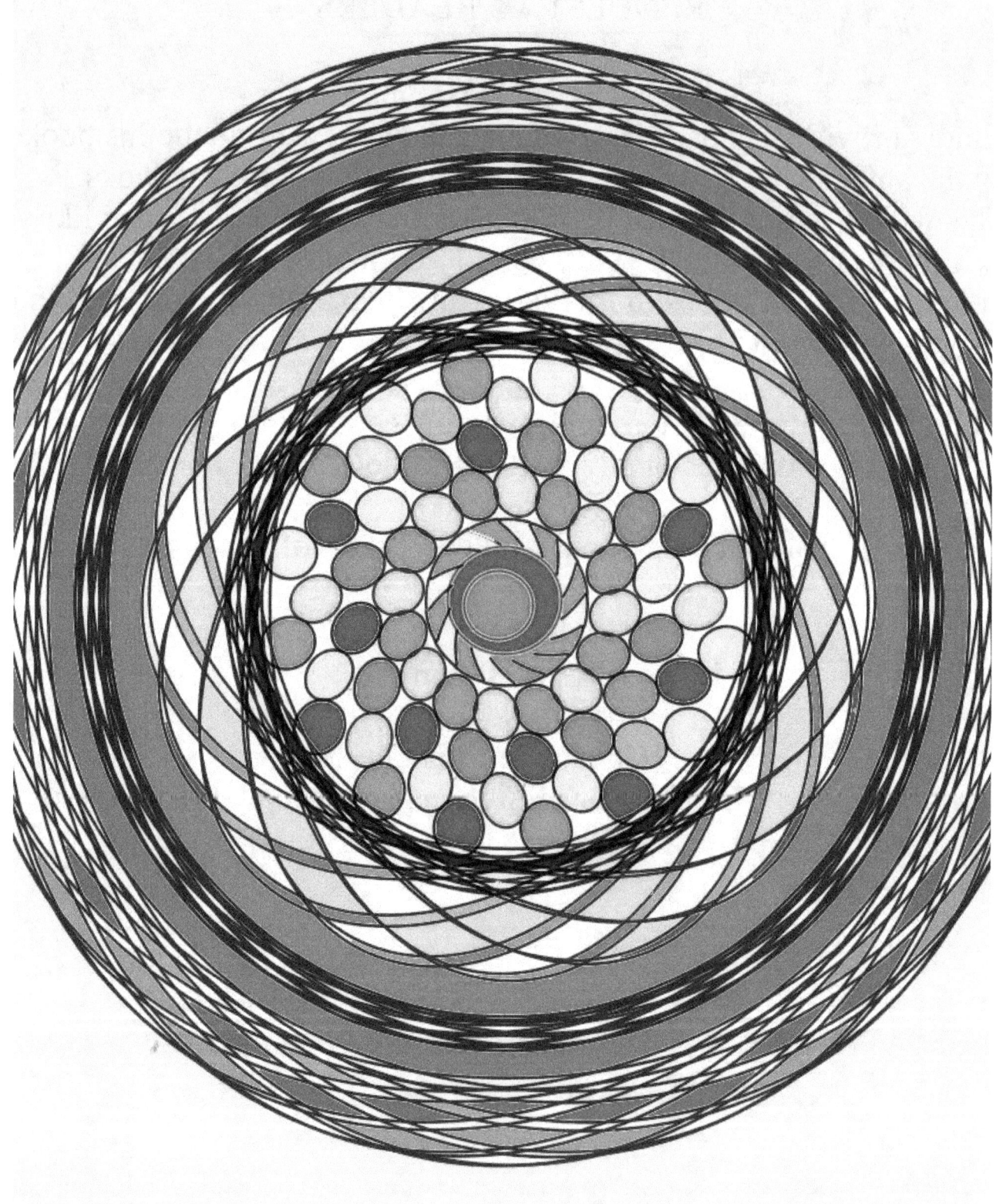

www.ingramcontent.com/pod-product-compliance
Lightning Source LLC
Chambersburg PA
CBHW082153230526
45467CB00044B/3212